Cheers and Praise for Dr. Grace Cornish and
10 Bad Choices That Ruin Black Women's Lives

"One of the finest self-help books available for women *and* men. Dr. Ruth, watch out, Dr. Laura, move over. Dr. Grace is in."

—*Atlanta Daily World*

"*10 Bad Choices* is a certified gold mine for African-American men and women looking for common-sense solutions to our relationship problems."

—Tony Patrick, *Black Men* magazine

"In a market full of gender war books, Dr. Grace stands out peacefully, daring to speak the truth about love and relationships. Her voice is a soothing blend of compassion, eloquence, wit, and charm."

—William July, author of *Brothers, Lust, and Love*

"Dr. Grace Cornish's unflinching belief that black men and women can, should—and, with the right tools, do—cherish one another informs her work. Her sassy, sisterly wisdom makes her a favorite with readers and television viewers."

—Claire McIntosh, senior editor, *Essence*

"*10 Bad Choices* is a must-read for women who want meaningful relationships. This book is insightful and very informative. It's important for us to read stories about women who have been there, done that!"

—Chrisena Coleman, author of *Just Between Girlfriends*

"Dr. Grace leaves no stone unturned with her truthful insights. Thorough, no-nonsense, savvy advice!"

—Debrena Jackson Gandy, author of *Sacred Pampering Principles*

"*10 Bad Choices* is a much-needed reality check and dose of tough love that should prove beneficial for women of all races."

—Kate Ferguson, editor in chief, *Today's Black Women*

"Three cheers for Dr. Grace Cornish for her wisdom, knowledge, and insight into the human conditions that nurture good, stable, male and female relationships. This is a must-read resource book capable of changing and enhancing relationships at any stage of development."

—Gilbert M. Lane, inventor of Flagships, a children's learning game

"This is a book every woman should read. It is spiritual, enlightening, educational, and it is *real*. It's like having your very own analyst in a tote bag."

—E. J. Davis, St. John Missionary Baptist Church, Chicago

"This book is a blueprint for black women who seek a balanced, healthy relationship."

—Dr. Rosie Milligan, author of
Satisfying Black Men/Women Sexually Made Simple

"An excellent healing tool for all women!"

—Donetta Dunbar, *Omaha World-Herald*

"Dr. Grace Cornish's book is a 'get real' document. She removes the idea that life is a dress rehearsal and puts the reader in charge of her selection process."

—Dr. Gwendolyn Goldsby Grant, author of
The Best Kind of Loving: A Black Woman's Guide to Finding Intimacy

"Dr. Grace gives us Sisters hope in the time of healing. Thank you, Grace, for helping us find our way."

—Rolanda Watts, entertainer and talk-show host

"*10 Bad Choices* is long overdue! Through it Dr. Grace empowers black women to make healthy relationship choices, with strong, honest, caring, and loving black men looking for the same."

—K. Thomas Oglesby, author of *What Black Men Should Do Now*

"This book frames what women need to be mindful of to reach the goal of romantic fulfillment."

—Dr. Sonia R. Banks, psychotherapist

"Dr. Cornish offers sound advice and welcome reminders on how to avoid the pitfalls that stand in the way of love—for ourselves and others."

—Yanick Rice Lamb, editorial director,
BET Weekend and *Heart & Soul* magazines

10

bad choices that ruin black women's lives

DR. GRACE CORNISH

THREE RIVERS PRESS • NEW YORK

Published by Three Rivers Press, New York, New York.
Member of the Crown Publishing Group.

Random House, Inc. New York, Toronto, London, Sydney, Auckland
www.randomhouse.com

THREE RIVERS PRESS is a registered trademark and the
Three Rivers Press colophon is a trademark of Random House, Inc.

Originally published in hardcover by Crown Publishers in 1998.

Printed in the United States of America

Design by Debbie Glasserman

Library of Congress Cataloging-in-Publication Data
Cornish, Grace.
10 bad choices that ruin black women's lives / by Dr. Grace Cornish.—1st ed.
1. African-American women—Life skills guides. 2. Man-woman relationships. I. Title.
E185.86.C582145   1998
305.48'896073—dc21   98-11062

ISBN 0-609-80133-3

10 9 8 7 6 5 4 3

This book is dedicated to you.

contents

preface

My mother's death is the foundation upon which this book was created. My beautiful, young, and compassionate mother was murdered by an obsessive and controlling ex-lover on July 11, 1972, one month shy of her twenty-ninth birthday. She was a gorgeous international runway and print model who was one of the first black women to model for the Paris-based fashion house Givenchy, the London-based Harrods department store, and New York–based Bloomingdale's department store. When she ended the relationship with her abusive lover, he shot her six times in the head. She died instantly. Then he reloaded the gun and killed himself. I was ten years old and witnessed the incident.

Twenty years later, my mother's sister, a smart, financially secure nurse, was also murdered by a jealous and controlling mate. He stabbed her repeatedly, forty times in all, on March 17, 1992, her fiftieth birthday.

Both my mother and Aunt Gloria were attractive, intelligent, and independent black women who made bad choices in their personal relationships that ultimately robbed them of their lives.

Today, far too many black women are still being robbed of wholesome and happy lives due to bad relationship choices. National statistics reflect that six out of every ten black women are in either poor relationships, man-sharing situations, or no relationship at all. This includes sisters from varying economic, educational, and social backgrounds. The problem is not the sisters themselves, but the bad choices they keep making for themselves.

My mother's death had a significant effect on me. At that

young age, I knew I would someday dedicate my life to helping people rid themselves of anxiety, despondency, and frustration and replace those feelings with hope, joy, and peace of mind. I didn't want anyone to lose their life like my mother had, or any child to feel the loss, pain, and detachment I experienced.

Aunt Gloria's death has inspired me even further. It led me to take a definite stand and carry out the responsibility of helping women and men improve their lives and prevent disaster by instilling in them self-worth, balance, and compatibility.

This book is designed to expose the emotional, social, and psychological roadblocks we unconsciously place in the way of our own success—and provide the tools for tearing down these barriers that are messing up or taking sisters' lives.

I hope that in reading this book you will discover that you are not alone, and that you will be able to free yourself from past disasters, correct present mistakes, and prevent future mishaps.

This book was written for you. It will guide you to successfully face and remove the obstacles that are keeping you from getting the healthy and loving relationship you deserve to have.

I wholeheartedly thank Crown Publishers for making this book possible. And especially Kristin Kiser, for her invaluable editorial expertise.

I deeply thank my agent, Jim Hornfischer, at The Literary Group International, for his wisdom and guidance.

To Helen Bungert, who always critiques my work and assists me in bringing out my best, I am forever grateful.

I thank Aunt D (Dureen McCalla), my "guardian" mother, for her unconditional, supportive, and nurturing love. She has molded my life and helped me to become the woman I am today. Through her I've learned how to truly give from the heart and how to love, purely and uncompromisingly.

My sincerest gratitude to my vibrant, loving, supportive sister, Angie: Thanks, Ang, for constantly believing in me, always looking out for my best interests, and forever cheering me on.

My fondest appreciation and love to my beautiful and mischievous little princess, Dena, who always brings a smile to my lips and laughter to my heart. God has truly blessed my life with her. My love to my nephew, Jason, for teaching me to have patience and understanding much deeper than I thought possible.

To my father, Clive: Thanks, Daddy, for the pep talks, and for essential briefings about men and relationships.

Heartfelt thanks to some wonderful and supportive friends: Heather Turnbull, Toni Gourdine, Liz Yasuda, Dr. Rosie Milligan, Margaret Grey, Mike Millis, Lingsworth Pendley, Norman Hall, Dr. Gwendolyn Goldsby Grant, Judith Gregory, and Adeyinka Adeola.

A word of thanks to some dynamic associates: Hazel Smith, D. Elaine Brown, Rayniece Holmes, Victoria Valentine, Avril Lacour, Sherri McGee, Connie Green, Milecent Cross, Juliette Fairley, Tracy E. Hopkins, Fritz Lewis, Monique Jellerette DeJongh, and Robbie Garrison.

Special thanks to my clients who have allowed me to share their stories in this book. And to the hundreds of participants from my workshops, seminars, and private consultations: Thanks for trusting me to be a beacon of light in your life.

And thanks to you who are reading this book for letting me into your life. Good for you, for making a sincere commitment to get rid of the old and bring in the new, and for choosing to enjoy your life to the fullest.

introduction

One of the most painful sights to see is an attractive, intelligent, smart, and hardworking black woman who is lonely and without a suitable man to keep her company; another is a well-rounded sister with a mismatched mate causing her grief. The question is, Why are so many black women alone or in bad relationships?

As a black woman facing many challenges on a daily basis—just surviving, working, paying bills, and building a career are major tasks—you cannot afford the added pressure of being unhappy in your love life. It's past time to awaken from the relationship nightmare. You deserve to have your own colorful version of the American Dream, complete with a companion who will complement you—one who will share your hopes, your dreams, your accomplishments, your laughter, and your tears—someone with whom you can have fun, wine and dine, take trips, grow, build a family, or just sit around and watch videos.

Sis, I am going to be completely realistic with you. This book will give you the tools you need to clear away the debris that has kept you from attracting the right love, but *you* have to be honest with yourself and be willing to take the necessary steps to improve your situation.

In my role as the advice columnist for the *New York Beacon,* a weekly newspaper, I have received numerous letters from black women and men who are desperately searching to make a compatible love connection but who have been unsuccessful, and from others who have thrown away potentially ideal relationships because of petty differences or bad choices.

The simple truth is that no man can stop you from being

happy unless you allow him to; it's your choice in men that has prevented you from being happy. Let's get to the heart of the matter, look at all the bad choices we have made, find out why, and fix them. We are going to *face them, erase them, and replace them.*

Society is quick to accept reports and statistics saying that black women are in a relationship dilemma because most black men are in jail or on drugs or subsisting at the poverty level. Sisters internalize these images and conclude that there are no eligible black men left—that the good ones are married, dead, or not yet born, and the rest are gay, bisexual, or interested only in white women. These are some of the most self-defeating misconceptions black women harbor. It is true that many brothers lack direction; however, to generalize this to all black men is both ridiculous and false.

There are many available black men who are single, straight, decent, successful, and looking for the right black woman. As for the issue of black men who prefer to be with women of other races, trust me: It's not as widespread as you are led to believe. The media has blown things way out of proportion. Don't be misled or discouraged by the propaganda. As a consulting expert for national TV, I can honestly tell you that a lot of the TV talk shows oversensationalize interracial relationships to instill fear and anger in order to boost their ratings. I'll give you more in-depth details further along in the book.

Instead of being distracted by who's with whom on a national level, each black woman must concentrate on scrutinizing her behavior on an individual level. In our relationships, believe it or not, we are the ones who most often block our own blessings without even knowing it.

An example: Tonya,* a thirty-five-year-old graphic artist, shared with me that she wanted to find and marry a successful and kind black man within a year. I advised her to let her friends

---

*Note: All names have been changed to protect each individual's right to privacy.

and coworkers know she's looking and have them scout around for a potential match. Within two weeks, one of her coworkers, who's happily married, said that her husband, a financial analyst, has a good friend and business partner who is single, successful, black, nice, available, and interested in meeting her.

Perfect, right? Wrong. Tonya, who's an attractive sister, claims she is "a little too overweight" and refuses to meet him until she loses some weight. But she has not consciously tried to lose any weight. It's been over three months now, and still she keeps postponing the meeting. Is Tonya throwing away a potential love connection? Certainly. She's blocking her own success and using her "weight problem" as an excuse.

Some sisters unconsciously use weight, fear, finance, status, skin coloring, and other barriers to keep themselves from getting the love they want. They are either choosing the wrong men for the wrong reasons or using unhealthy excuses to deprive themselves of choosing the right men. This book will give you a clear picture of how black women miss out on success because of mistaken goals, insecurities, and bad relationship choices. It will provide effective prescriptions for positive change—change that builds a solid foundation for a better sense of self, better relationships, and better choices.

I've spent the past several years working with men and women, finding out what makes relationships succeed and what causes them to fail. I've made a few bad choices myself, but I'm happy to say that I not only survived the difficult and sometimes painful voyage, but I've used my valuable experience to help many others correct and prevent bad choices and find the loving relationships they have been looking for.

Throughout this book I will share with you my personal stories as well as the stories of other women and men from my private consultations, my consultations on national TV talk shows, my advice column in the *New York Beacon,* and material from my national workshops and seminars. Some of the stories may sadden you, others may amuse you, some may anger you, and many may shock you, but all will certainly have an important impact on your life and give you a candid picture of the *10 Bad Choices That Ruin Black Women's Lives.*

I hope this book will help you get to the core of your personal situation and make the right choice so that you finally enjoy a rewarding and enriching life.

You deserve happiness, sis. Don't deprive yourself.

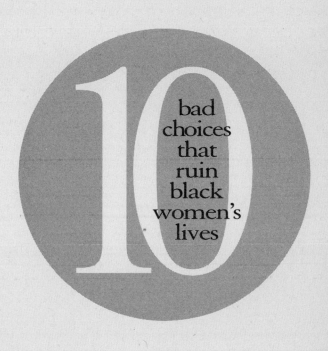

10 bad choices that ruin black women's lives

bad choice

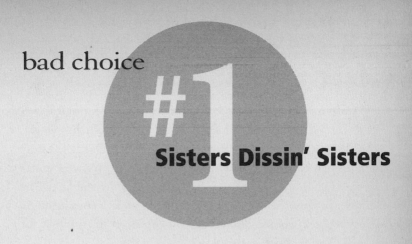

#1

Sisters Dissin' Sisters

Have you ever wondered why so many sisters choose to be so competitive with and disrespectful of each other?

Overall, the sisterhood among black women is a very good support system. However, too many sisters purposefully belittle, disgrace, and undermine each other.

The purpose of this book is twofold: First, to ensure that black women are respected in their relationships on an individual level; and second, to ensure that black women are more respected in society at large on a collective level. But how can we be respected on any level if we don't take the initiative and respect each other on a personal level?

I knew I had to begin this book by addressing the deplorable practice of sisters dissin' sisters, and I can remember the particular incident that made me even more determined to speak about this topic. A few years ago, while promoting my last book, *Radiant Women of Color,* I was invited to be the guest expert on a major TV talk show. The producer, a black woman, said that she needed me as a self-esteem expert for her show, to discuss how the Barbie doll affects women and their self-images. She explained that there would be both black and white women on the panel and that she needed me to speak about self-worth for all women. That sounded decent enough.

A few hours later the producer called me again and said that she was working on another show simultaneously. She asked if I knew any black men who dated white women exclusively. I told her I didn't. Then she asked if I knew of any who had dated white women in the past. I told her that the only such person I could think of offhand was my sister's neighbor, Darnell, a very frivolous playboy bachelor who dates women of all races, sometimes two or three at a time. I also added that he might not be available because he was presently involved in a love triangle with two black women. She asked if I could get his number for her. I did and thought nothing further of it.

The next day when I arrived at the studio for the taping of the "Barbie doll" show, I was brought to the greenroom to watch the show's progress until it was my turn to go on, toward the end of the show.

The show started harmlessly enough as the male host, holding up a white Barbie doll, announced, "It's been on the market for over thirty years and it's the best-selling, most popular doll on the planet, but as its popularity has grown, so has the debate over this piece of plastic's impact on female self-perception." I began to get a very uneasy feeling as he continued, now holding up a black Barbie doll: "On today's show, black women and white women *fight* over the Barbie doll image."

The word "fight" did not sit well with me at all. There we were, women, black and white, who faced enough challenges every day just being women, placed in an arena so that others could watch us compete against and antagonize each other. The first set of guests introduced were three attractive white women who wanted to look like Barbie, one of whom had spent over seventy-five thousand dollars on plastic surgery. The next set of guests were three attractive black women. Two of these women had no intention of looking like Barbie. But the other, a twenty-year-old sister, Deidre, wanted to get a nose job to look like Barbie. Here's an example of how she was exploited by the host and audience alike:

DEIDRE: I would do anything to get a nose job. I need my black nose done today.

HOST: I don't want to put words in your mouth, but are you saying that having white European features will help?

DEIDRE: Yes. I'm called ugly by my own kind. My own sister calls me pig nose, pug nose. I don't even go out. I am twenty years old and the only place I go is to school. And I only go there because I have to. When I take pictures, my nose covers the whole picture.

At this point the audience laughed hysterically, not realizing the pain this young woman was harboring. She started getting teary-eyed, struggling to hide her pain. Then the host instigated a heated debate between the black and white women on the stage. He went to a commercial break, leaving the audience with, "Next, a black man who says these black women can learn a lot from these Barbies."

During this time I was still in the greenroom, not believing the chaos that was going on out there and wondering what in the world this black-woman producer had been thinking when she'd put this show together—and what having a black man onstage had to do with these women's self-image problems. As if black women didn't have enough troubles—how dare this sister-producer belittle other black women in this way! But it got worse as the show progressed. I was not prepared for what followed.

HOST: We're back. My next guest says that Barbie represents the real woman and that's why he won't date a black woman. Meet Darnell. Darnell, why do you feel this way?

It was Darnell, my sister's neighbor. The unstable lover boy who was currently involved with not one, but two, black women was going to lie about his interest in black women because he had been talked into it by the producer—a black woman. I couldn't believe it. At this point I became disgusted.

HOW LOW WILL ONE GO FOR FIFTEEN MINUTES OF "FAME"?

DARNELL: Well *(Pause)*, basically, I've dated a large spectrum of women, and what I find is that white women will do more for the black man than black women overall . . .

HOST: Well, you've dated black women in the past . . .

DARNELL: Yes.

HOST: Describe a black woman to me.

DARNELL: Well, a black woman, she'll do a lot for you and everything *(Nervous and contradicting himself because he's lying)*, but she won't do for herself. I mean, as far as exercising and taking care of her body, or going to health clubs, it's not happening . . . *(At this point the audience is extremely angry and is hurling unsolicited remarks at him)*

HOST: *(To the audience)* Wait, wait. I want to hear the rest of the story. Let the man finish. *(To Darnell)* Well, is it just about her looks and how she takes care of herself? *(Points to the white women on the panel)* These ladies here, do they represent more of what you'd be interested in dating?

DARNELL: There you go! Exactly!

HOST: Are you saying that Susie and the other two white women are your ideal?

DARNELL: Exactly. But, I mean, these black women onstage look fine, but they don't represent all black women.

HOST: *(Continues to stoke the fire)* Well, Darnell, give me three words to describe the bulk of black women.

DARNELL: Well, I mean, they have good traits. These are fine . . .

HOST: No, no. What's the problem with black women? I want to know the other side.

DARNELL: *(Nervously stalling)* Well, in some instances it's laziness, not [being] goal-oriented. These look fine, but on the whole a lot of black women are tacky . . .

That did it! One of the black women on the stage told him off in a thorough and dignified manner, the audience went wild, and Darnell was removed from the stage.

To try to restore order, the host quickly switched back to the original topic about women and self-image.

HOST: Ladies, ladies, please calm down. I'd like to go ahead and introduce my next guest. My next guest teaches women of all colors how to free themselves from the pressures of being pretty. Meet the best-selling author of *Radiant Women of Color,* Dr. Grace Cornish. Dr. Cornish, are Susie and the others too caught up in their looks?

DR. CORNISH: First of all, before I answer anything, I'd like to say there's beauty in all women, whether of Caucasian, Asian, Hispanic, Indian, or African descent . . .

HOST: *(Interrupting, trying to lead me down his ridiculous path)* Without changing anything about themselves?

COMPARISON IS AN UGLY PRACTICE

DR. CORNISH: Wait a minute. Just hold on a second. I'm going to emphasize that. This show has already gotten off the main topic. It shouldn't have become a black-against-white issue. No one race of people is ugly; the only thing that's ugly is comparison. When we compare one race to another, that's when we get into trouble and damage people's minds. *(Audience applause)*

HOST: But, but . . . *(At this point, he's obviously lost and searching for something to sway me)* But, the clothes you are wearing are European . . . *(Don't ask where this came from. I guess he was trying to entrap me, but I refused to be sidetracked by the ridiculous tactic)*

DR. CORNISH: *(Interrupting the host)* I am not going to go there! I am not going to let you put me there. *(To the panel and the* *young black sister who was hurting)* Ideal beauty is learning to feel good about yourself, no matter what you choose to do with your individual package. The Creator has given you a mind, a body, and a spirit, and no one on this earth has any right to belittle or dictate how another should look. God is your Creator, and you are a gift from Him. Beauty, true beauty, is a totality, it's a totality . . . *(Audience applause)*

HOST: *(Upset because I wouldn't take his bait)* Okay, okay, I hear ya . . .

DR. CORNISH: *(To host)* Just a minute. *(To panel)* Don't ever let anyone set an ideal for you. Your beauty is as individual as you are. True beauty is a balance—you have to have a balance. *(Audience applause)*

HOST: *(Abruptly)* I'm sorry, we're out of time. I think you are all beautiful. Thanks to all my guests for being on today's show. See you next time.

At the end of the taping, the executives and crew congratulated the host: "Good show. Excellent energy."

What a circus act. This callous and cold treatment of women was simply business as usual to them. Nothing more, nothing less. After the show the young black sister, Deidre, cried hysterically. I spent half an hour trying to calm her down. She kept repeating, "I didn't know it would be like this. All I wanted was a nose job. I didn't know they would laugh at me."

The sister-producer who was responsible for putting this degrading nonsense together was nowhere around. One of her assistants saw me calming Deidre down and came over to me and said, "Is she going to be okay? Thanks so much for being here today. You did a great job out there. The audience loved you."

I was taken aback by the staff and crew's nonchalance toward the young sister's pain. I asked the producer's assistant directly, "What was all that about? How could you guys twist the show like that?"

She very casually responded, "Marketing. Don't worry about it. It's the nature of the business."

I was livid. "You mean to tell me you people have caused this girl such pain, and talked that man into lying, just because of marketing?"

She looked at me as if I was overreacting and simply remarked, "It's just a show."

That show was the only bad experience I've had in all my years of consulting for television. And at that moment I was very sad. I was sad because no one cared that the experience would possibly mess up that young black woman's life.

I shook my head in disappointment and said as I left; "You know, this is the perfect example of people who are selling their souls in an attempt to gain the world."

DON'T TRY TO GET ON TOP BY PUTTING YOUR SISTERS ON THE BOTTOM

You may wonder why I was more upset at the black woman instead of the black man. As women we have to be more conscious of our own self-images. Given that brother's track record and his deceptive behavior, we see that he was a foolish man who would have done or said anything to get on TV. As a matter of fact, he's an embarrassment to the images of decent black men. The sister, however, held a substantial position in the media. What she produces on television goes directly into the homes, hearts, and minds of millions of viewers on a daily basis. She should have made it her responsibility not to promote the damaging filth that has daubed black women for far too long. But instead, she chose to titillate viewers and boost her ratings by sensationalizing and exploiting the images of black women and by creating racial tension.

So, yes, I was very ashamed of this sister who chose to disrespect black women across America. A bad choice indeed. But as we all know, "God don't love ugly." And when you cause harm to another, sooner or later you are bound to suffer yourself. It's the universal law of cause and effect. Whatever goes around comes around.

That talk show was canceled after that season. It didn't surprise me at all. However, several months later, the sister-producer relocated to another major city to work on another major national TV talk show. I was told that she invited the same guy, Darnell, to repeat the same type of program. And again her show folded within one year. No surprise there, either. People are getting tired of seeing this degrading nonsense on TV.

Do you think that sister will ever wake up and get with the *real* program? When sisters disrespect sisters they damage the essential fiber that holds the black community together. To share a quote from my own book, *Radiant Women of Color*, "We are all in this oversized boat together, and whether we sink or survive depends on how well we can paddle together."

STICKS AND STONES WILL BREAK THE BONES, AND HARSH WORDS WILL BREAK A SISTER'S SPIRIT

How often have we bad-mouthed other sisters or laughed while others did the bad-mouthing? Whether we join in the conversation or listen in silence, we are at fault for not putting a stop to it. Must we continue to use our words as weapons to harm instead of remedies to heal?

Do any of these statements sound familiar?

1. "She thinks she's all that, but she ain't."
2. "I can't believe he's with her."
3. "How the hell did she get him?"
4. "It should be me on his arm instead of her."
5. "I know she ain't wearing that dress."
6. "She's too dark for that."
7. "Check out girlfriend's weave."
8. "Now, I know she didn't go blond."

9. "She needs to grow some hair."
10. "She is just jealous of me."

These words hurt people's feelings, and the following ten statements do not excuse us when we put each other down:

1. "I was only joking."
2. "But it's the truth."
3. "Everybody already knows it."
4. "She'll never find out about it."
5. "I'd say the same thing even if she was here."
6. "I wouldn't mind if someone said it about me."
7. "I did the same thing myself."
8. "We're friends, so she won't mind."
9. "I didn't actually say anything bad about her."
10. "I didn't mean any harm."

How Low Will a Sister Go?

Deliberate betrayal from other sisters is one of the major reasons why black women have such a difficult time in relationships. This by no means excuses the behavior of the man involved, but it is generally the woman who dictates a relationship. In other words, if a man makes an advance toward a woman and she tells him that she is not interested, he has no choice but to back off.

Although many men very often lie about being involved with someone else, some women are intrigued by the "thrill" of sneaking around with another sister's man. For some reason, many sisters feel special if they are able to steal a man's attention from another sister.

A classic example of the damaging effect and danger of one sister betraying another sister in this way is the scenario of two former best friends—thirty-nine-year-old Cybil and thirty-seven-year-old Beverly.

Cybil and Beverly had known each other for over seven years.

When Beverly's abusive live-in boyfriend beat her, blinded her in one eye, almost killed her, and threw her out of their house, she had no place to go. Cybil took her into her home to live with her family.

The two women grew closer, and Beverly became the god-mother of Cybil's third child. After a while, Cybil's husband of nineteen years began to treat her badly and distance himself from her. He had cheated on her numerous times in the past, and she suspected he was having another affair, but when she confronted him, he denied it. Beverly kept telling her to leave him.

THERE IS JUST NO EXCUSE FOR THIS . . .

After eighteen months, the truth came out. Cybil's sixteen-year-old daughter came home from school early one afternoon and caught her father and Beverly having sex in Cybil's bedroom. She immediately called her mother at work.

Beverly had the nerve to stay until Cybil got home. When Cybil confronted her, she sarcastically said, "I didn't go after him. He came after me," and "If you were doing what you were supposed to be doing, he wouldn't have had to seek another woman." In anger, Cybil screamed "Woman? You are no real woman—you are nothing but a one-eyed bitch!" Without even the slightest remorse, Beverly answered, "So what? If I can take your man with only one eye, can you imagine what I would take with two?" Cybil attacked her, and the police had to be called in to break up the fight.

What a mess! Women like Beverly, who have no morals and no respect for themselves or others, are messed-up human beings who end up messing up other people's lives. Misery truly loves company.

Cybil kicked Beverly out of her house, but her husband refuses to leave. They sleep in separate bedrooms, and he still continues to see Beverly outside the home. Cybil has filed for divorce, and as soon as the house is sold, she'll take her share of the money and start a new life for herself and her children.

When Cybil first came to see me she was at a very low point and was considering suicide. She was very distraught, and justifiably so, but as time went on I managed to convince her that nothing and no one is worth losing her life over or taking her away from her three beautiful children.

To me, one of the biggest pities is that she didn't get rid of her husband long ago, since he cheated on her so often in the past. By acting earlier she could have saved herself and her children a lot of pain. She is doing much better today, but it's going to take some time before she learns to trust again.

DON'T THANK A SISTER WITH A ROTTEN DEED IF SHE HAS HELPED YOU WHEN YOU WERE IN NEED

Sisters like Beverly need intensive therapy. To betray your friend's trust and sleep with her man is cruelty enough, but to add insult to injury by doing it in her own bed is pathetic. This is the betrayal of all betrayals. When Cybil's dysfunctional, soon-to-be-ex–husband starts to cheat on Beverly (and he will), I hope she'll remember the pain and damage she has caused this kindhearted sister and her children.

IT'S NO CHALLENGE TO SHARE A SISTER'S MAN; THE REAL CHALLENGE IS GETTING A GOOD MAN ON YOUR OWN

Twenty-five-year-old Lorna and twenty-one-year-old LaKeisha provide another example of sisters who disrespect other sisters openly and without regret. While taping an episode of *Ricki Lake* called "I Say Your Man Is Fair Game; Watch Out, Girl, I'm on a Mission," these sisters proudly declared that they have no shame when it comes to taking another sister's man.

As a matter of fact, they were rather proud of their conquests.

Lorna especially was extremely vocal and was pleased to share that she doesn't think twice about hitting on another woman's man, even if the woman is a friend or her actual blood sister.

When the host, Ricki, asked Lorna if any man was off-limits, she said no and added with glee, "I use my looks to take *any* woman's man I want. I take their money. I use them. And too bad who don't like it."

When her friend, Tamara, shared, "There's enough guys out here for us to have our own," Lorna interjected, "It's just the challenge of getting yours, and there's nothing you can do about it. I have already taken two of yours, and I'll take any more I see you with if I want to."

A woman in the audience called her a slut, and she responded, "I may be one, but I'm a damn good one and a highly paid one. And if I want your man I will take him too." Lorna carried on disgracefully, and no one could get a word in edgewise.

After the commercial break, Ricki asked for my advice. I told Lorna and LaKeisha that any woman who doesn't have enough confidence to get her own man, but settles for yo-yoing from man to man, has a serious problem. The audience applauded favorably as I continued, "What this is doing is giving you ladies a false sense of challenge. The real challenge is whether you can come out here and brag that you have a man who's making a commitment to you and only you. Then I will applaud you, but now you are only bouncing from man to man. Your behavior cheapens you. Any man can find behavior like yours on any corner of New York City for five or ten dollars."

BEING LOOSE IS NOTHING TO BRAG ABOUT

Lorna toned her antics down a bit and said, "I'm not trying to disrespect anyone out here. I'm just me and I'm not gonna change, no matter what nobody says. It's my choice."

I told Lorna that she was right as far as it being her choice, but she was wrong if she believed she wasn't disrespecting anyone. "You know what's bad about your choice?" I asked. "You feel pleased at being labeled a slut. That's self-defeating. Any woman can become a slut if she chooses to. It's the oldest profession in the world. However, challenge yourself to find your own man, a decent man, and attempt to stay in that relationship with one man for at least six months, and see how it will change your life."

IS THIS THE CODE OF THE SISTERHOOD?

I was told that after this episode aired, the phone rang off the hook at *Ricki Lake*. Lorna had struck a nerve in women all over the country. Both married women and live-in girlfriends called seeking effective solutions and coping skills to deal with the messes the Lornas of the world were making in their lives. Surprisingly enough, quite a few of the mistresses also called seeking help.

This particular program encouraged a lot of women to come forward and get the help they needed. I'll share some of their heartrending stories with you a little later, when I discuss Bad Choice #7, "Loving the 'Married Bachelor.'"

WANT TO SUCCEED IN LIFE? USE YOUR MIND, NOT YOUR BEHIND

Black women have come a long way. But with sisters still disrespecting and competing with each other for men, we clearly have a long way to go. As I always tell my clients, you should never *copy, compare,* or *compete.* Instead, you should *condition*—condition yourself to become the best that you can be.

What the Lornas out there don't realize is that when they mess up their sisters' lives, they also, directly or indirectly, mess up their own. For you sisters who are wallowing in the negativity of dissin' and competing with your sisters, you need to take that competitive streak out of your sister's bedroom, take it into the boardroom or the classroom, and become a decent citizen in the black community and in society at large. Then you'll be able to attract a worthwhile and upstanding man of your own.

BLAMING ANOTHER SISTER WILL NOT MAKE YOUR PROBLEMS GO AWAY: YOU'VE GOT TO GET TO THE REAL ISSUES

Thirty-eight-year-old Shelly wanted to use black magic and voodoo in hopes of harming Brenda, a coworker.

Shelly and Brenda worked for the same department in a large advertising firm. Shelly had been employed by the company for nine years, and thirty-three-year-old Brenda had been employed there for two years. They were both assigned to the same campaign team. Shelly had become complacent in her job. She would watch the clock and count down the hours until it was time to go home. Brenda, on the other hand, was a fiery go-getter who often stayed late after work to improve her assignments. When Shelly was passed up in favor of Brenda for a promotion, Shelly was angry.

Shelly had a crush on her boss, Thomas, but he never showed any interest. After Brenda's promotion, Brenda and Thomas started dating seriously. Shelly became even angrier.

I met Shelly while conducting a time-management and stress-control seminar for the advertising company. After the program she approached me, introduced herself, and asked if I had a few minutes to talk to her. I said yes. She started out by sharing that she felt overstressed at work and felt frustrated because she was getting nowhere. Before she had a chance to continue, Brenda and another coworker stopped briefly to thank me for the seminar.

Shelly gave Brenda a very nasty look and when Brenda was out of earshot, mumbled, "I hate that bitch."

"Excuse me—what did you say?" I asked. I knew what I had heard, but I just wanted to make sure.

"Nothing," she responded.

"Shelly, I heard you. What's the matter? Why do you hate her?"

Shelly felt comfortable with me and told me about Brenda, Thomas, and the promotion. She said she felt that Brenda had taken what should have been hers. I asked her if she really liked her job and if she had been trying her best in order to get the promotion. She paused, and when I told her to be honest with herself, she responded, "I didn't put my all into it." I told her that Brenda didn't take the job away from her, but that she (Shelly) gave it away from the very beginning by not putting her best forward. And she couldn't blame Brenda for Thomas's romantic decision, either.

It was if Shelly didn't hear a word I said. "I still can't stand Brenda," she repeated. She added that one of her friends had given her some ads from a national black hair magazine that promised to use "powerful roots to conquer your enemies and control a lover."

When I heard this, I immediately interjected, " 'Powerful roots'? What you need is powerful *prayer* in your life. Instead of wanting to use roots in an attempt to control someone's life, what you need to use is some good old-fashioned grassroots prayer to communicate with the holy spirit of God to gain control of your own life. Don't even think of destroying yourself like that."

GET TO KNOW YOURSELF SO YOU CAN LEARN TO LOVE YOURSELF

As the conversation continued, I found out that Shelly's real problem was not her hatred for Brenda; it was her hatred for herself— self-hatred she wasn't even aware of. She shared that all her life she'd been called "ugly, tar baby, nappy-head, and bug-eyes." She had attended an all-black university where the sisters on campus were very discriminating and unkind, and she had always felt like an outsider.

I explained to her that Brenda wasn't her enemy, that the real enemies were the awful memories inside her, and that in order to fix her life she had to be willing to deal with the past experiences instead of just burying them. When this work was done, she would be able to attract the right job and the right relationship for her.

Shelly said she was ready to improve her life. The following week she went through my Know Thyself/Love Thyself program as described in my book *Radiant Women of Color.* The first thing she did was to stop blaming Brenda. Within a few weeks, Shelly literally became a new person. And guess what? She apologized to Brenda, and they get along very well now. After three months, she received an excellent job offer, which she accepted. As far as finding a love relationship, she told me that she's still working on it and that she can't wait to get her hands on this book.

You will be surprised by what you can accomplish when you take an honest look at your life, take full responsibility for your setbacks as well as your successes, and stop blaming others for "hard times" or "bad breaks." It's very easy to point a finger at someone else, as Shelly did to Brenda. But the sooner you choose to be the writer of your own life script, the sooner you can improve your life's direction.

HEY, SIS, HOW ABOUT CONFRONTING THE SILENT MAN IN THE MIDDLE?

How many stories have you heard, or how many talk shows have you seen, where sisters are quick to tear each other apart instead of dealing with a two-timing mate? All too often the man sits silently in the center, feeling like a prized Casanova, while the women involved degrade each other.

Sisters, we've got to stop this habit of disrespecting each other. Men can sense the rifts we've created among us. Brothers know that a lot of sisters do not trust each other, and believe me, they use it to their own advantage. That's why they'll go out with a

Trina, a Gina, and a Nina at the same time and not worry at all. In one of my workshops, one Casanova proudly boasted that he "shuffles women like a deck of cards." When asked why, he simply said, "Because women let me get away with it."

By the way, for the brothers who are either sneaking a peek at or openly reading this book, you can put down your guard, because this is not a man-bashing book, and I am not a man-bashing female psychologist. As a matter of fact, my entire purpose is to improve communications and relationships between black men and women. But in order to do so successfully, the truth must be dealt with openly. And if you are one of the decent and good black men, you certainly will not take offense at my getting to the heart of the matter. Most likely you'll be relieved as I expose the reckless lover boys who give black men a rotten name and black women a rotten game.

I've appeared on *Rolonda* numerous times as the guest expert. During the taping of the episode "What Are You Looking At? He's Mine," two sisters almost had a physical fight over a man. It was sheer madness. One of the young women was his girlfriend and the other sister was his best friend. The girlfriend complained that his best friend was always "hugging, kissing, and hanging all over him," and said that it had to end immediately because she wasn't going to put up with it anymore.

When Rolonda asked the best friend if this was true, she boldly responded, "Yes." When asked why, she answered, "I do it because I know it bothers her. He and I have been friends for ten years. We are just friends, but no one is going to come between us in our friendship." The brother was so pleased with the fact that the two sisters were battling over him that he was actually grinning from ear to ear, like the Cheshire cat.

When an audience member asked why he didn't put a stop to the rivalry between the two women, he shrugged his shoulders and said with a big smile on his face, "What can I do? I'm caught in the middle. Let them work it out."

WHY REDUCE YOURSELF TO THIS?

At that point the show became very chaotic. The girlfriend had extension braids; she tied them up and was ready to fight. Rolonda had to really put her foot down to get the rivals to quiet down. She did an excellent job, really making them stop and think, and adding, "Once again, the man is in the middle without saying a word." She declared that she would like to see more women respecting each other, woman to woman. Then she introduced me and asked me about my approach of holistic relationship therapy.

I responded, "Holistic relationship therapy is coming into relationships from the mind, body, and spirit. From what I've heard here today, it's only about the physical, about lust and about possession. I've not heard anyone say anything about trust, respect, or love. *(Audience applause)* I've not heard it. Isn't that what a relationship is all about? It's about love. Respectful love. Let me tell you something: If something is truly yours, it can never be taken away from you."

Rolonda enthusiastically asked me to reemphasize the importance of respectful and compatible love. I repeated it, the audience appreciated it, the girlfriend untied her braids, and the show ended on a positive note.

I sincerely hope those sisters went home and took a good look at that tape, realized how badly they had carried on, and chose to improve their future behavior. Most of all, I hope they discovered that disrespecting each other is not the answer. Hopefully they will deal with the puppetmaster "boyfriend" and stop allowing him to manipulate them, before they ruin their reputations and mess up their lives further.

WHEN IN DOUBT, LEAVE HER OUT

Have you ever had a friend who was very supportive in every area of your life except for the man department? It's a common joke around sisters that when it comes to relationships, "All brothers are guilty until proven innocent." But what about the girlfriends who openly solicit affairs? I have gotten many letters from sisters asking how to deal with friends whom they can trust with their lives, but not with their lovers.

If you need to question your man's fidelity, you probably need to get a new man. But we'll talk about that in the following chapters. Right now let's talk about how to handle the soliciting girlfriend. There are different levels of friendship. You can like someone but dislike her actions. If you have a friend you enjoy spending time with, but believe you can't trust her, instead of dissolving the friendship, just keep her as a "friendly acquaintance." Continue to enjoy selected activities with her, like shopping or going to the movies or museums, but if a situation arises where she might interfere with your love life, just leave her at home.

BEING LABELED AS A "SISTER TO AVOID" IS NO BADGE OF HONOR

Here's a letter I ran in my advice column in the *New York Beacon:*

Dear Dr. Cornish:

I have a close friend who is very supportive, kind and caring. She is a 40-year-old beautician, who doesn't look a day over 30. We've known each other for over six years and have always helped each other through all kinds of problems.

The problem is she has one major flaw—she turns into the world's biggest flirt when men are around. It's not just light flirtation, but heavy take-me-to-bed signals. When an attractive man is anywhere in sight, she instantly transforms from a well-together sister, into a loose, non-caring woman. She'll be the first on line to support a friend or anyone in need, but also the first to sleep with anyone's man she wants. How can someone who is so kind in one area be so unkind in another?

E. L., New York, NY

Dear E. L.:

Many people have different weaknesses in life. Your friend happens to be addicted to attractive men. Unfortunately, she takes it a bit too far by "sleeping with anyone's man she wants." This is an obsessive flaw that is sure to wreck both her reputation and her self-respect. Generally, people tend to be loose when they are searching for some sort of inner completion.

Her excessive flirting provides a false fulfillment for her deeply ingrained hunger for attention. In her mind, this gives her a sense of importance and validation.

She seems to be a very compassionate person who has some major issues to face and correct. As a child, she may have been neglected or ill-treated. Or, maybe she is just a vain woman who loves to solicit admiration, sexual or otherwise, from anyone who will acknowledge her.

Either way, this thirst for attention is both destructive and harmful. As a friend, you should speak with her openly about her behavior. Let her know you are concerned about her and don't want to see her get hurt. If she's not willing to curb her actions, continue to be her friend, but be very careful where you go with her.

TRUST HAS TO BE EARNED

If you truly feel you cannot trust a particular woman in the company of men, based on her own actions, then don't. Check yourself first, to make sure you are not just being insecure or paranoid, but if you are sure, go with your woman's intuition. As the saying goes, "An ounce of prevention is better than a pound of cure." Remember Cybil's example. Although she probably would have eventually divorced her cheating husband anyway, it would have been much less messy if there had not been a double betrayal, with the "accomplice in grime" being her onetime friend.

IF YOU HAVE A TRUSTWORTHY GIRLFRIEND, DON'T DUMP HER AS SOON AS YOU GET A MAN

I want to close this chapter on a positive note about the importance of sisters respecting each other. It is very important to have a support circle of good girlfriends, even if that circle consists of only two or three other sisters. It's an age-old truth that good friends are very hard to find.

Here's a story I'd like to share:

Thirty-four-year-old Lauren and thirty-six-year-old Janice were close friends since college. They both attended school in Atlanta, and both majored in playwriting.

After college they went to opposite coasts to start their careers. Lauren's job took her to the East Coast, with the allure of Broadway, while Janice's led her to the West Coast, with the thrill of Hollywood.

They've always kept in touch over the years. After Lauren and Janice had been apart for four years, Lauren relocated to Los Angeles and embarked on a promising career as an in-house writer for a major motion-picture company. The two friends became roommates and reestablished a very close sister bond. By this time Janice had a lucrative position as a writer for a popular television sitcom. She worked with a team of six writers headed by Craig, a very handsome, charming, and single thirty-nine-year-old brother.

One day Lauren went by Janice's office to pick her up. When Craig saw her, he was immediately smitten. Janice introduced them. The next day he told Janice he'd like to date Lauren and asked her to put in a good word for him. She did. Soon after, Craig and Lauren started dating, and they soon became an item. They moved in together after three months.

WHY ALLOW YOURSELF TO BE PRESSURED INTO LOSING A GOOD FRIEND?

Craig complained that Lauren spent too much time with Janice, so Lauren began distancing herself from her friend. She went from seeing Janice twice a week to seeing her just two Thursdays per month. Janice, of course, was very hurt by this. She had other friends, so she kept herself busy, but Lauren was supposed to be her best friend.

Lauren then informed Janice that Craig had said he'd "prefer" her to stop seeing Janice on their two Thursdays because he wanted Lauren's undivided attention "just because he loved her so much."

At that point Janice's anger erupted, and she lashed out, "Why are you letting this man make your decisions? Can't you think for yourself?" Lauren retorted, "You should be happy for me instead of being jealous."

At this point the friendship dissolved. Soon Craig became verbally and physically abusive to Lauren. She hadn't questioned his controlling nature or his need to isolate her from her friends. She had mistakenly believed it was love. She now felt that she was trapped and had no one to turn to for help. She was very embarrassed at having dumped her friend ten months before. She wanted out but felt she couldn't call Janice after the way she'd treated her, and she was too ashamed to let her family know.

A SISTER IN NEED IS A SISTER INDEED

On Christmas Eve that year, Craig beat Lauren badly and stormed out of the house. She felt as if she was dying but was afraid to report him to the police, not knowing what he would do to her in return.

As fate would have it, Janice, who wasn't aware of any of this, decided to try to make peace for the holidays, so after a long deliberation, she called Lauren to wish her well. After seven rings, Lauren reluctantly answered the phone, trying to conceal the torment in her voice. At first she tried to pretend all was well, but when she heard the comforting voice of the good friend she had cast aside, she broke down and asked for help.

Janice didn't have to think twice; she immediately went to her friend's rescue, getting her out of the house and away from danger. It took some time for Lauren to get through her bad memories of Craig, but Janice was there to help her. And not once did she say "I told you so." However, she did say "Don't ever lose communication with your friends again."

A Genuine Friend Is a Precious Commodity

The moral of Lauren and Janice's story is: Never let a good friend go for anyone. I hope by now you realize how rare, priceless, and important trustworthy friends are. So don't disregard them as soon as you get into a new relationship. Even though you almost certainly won't be spending the same amount of time together, you should still keep in touch. I cannot overemphasize the importance of always having a supportive bond with sister-friends, even if the bond is with only one or two others.

Lauren dropped her girlfriend because her controlling lover told her she was infringing on his time. A well-balanced man will never isolate you from your trustworthy friends. In obeying Craig, Lauren discarded a valuable friendship. This was a bad choice on her part, and it could eventually have cost her her life, had her friend not saved her in time. She's fortunate she was able to get out with the help of her friend.

Millions of women, my mother and my aunt included, have not been spared, because no one knew. I'll share their stories when I discuss Bad Choice #6, "Staying On, Although Respect Has Gone," I hope this will either help you get out, help you to help a friend out, or prevent you from going into an isolating and unhealthy union.

In the meantime, don't disrespect your sister; she could be the very one to someday save your life.

bad choice 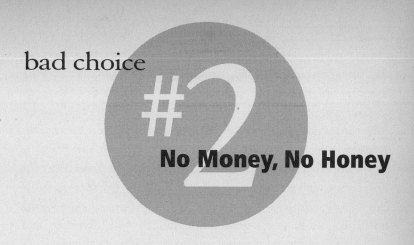#2

No Money, No Honey

If you ask most women what the first quality is that they look for in a man, they'll say he should be rich. Sisters are no different. Now, I'm the first to cheer you on and to coach you in going for the best in life, but I'm also the first to tell you that if you choose a man by the contents of his wallet instead of by his character, you are choosing foolishly.

Many sisters fantasize about meeting and marrying a rich black man who will "take care" of them. Many others have given up hope of marriage and would be happy to share a rich black man, so long as he takes care of the bills. Still others have chosen to cross the color line in search of a rich *any* man because, in their own words, they are tired of "the poor-ass black men who can't do a damn thing for them."

IF YOU WANT YOUR SLICE OF THE AMERICAN PIE, THEN HELP TO BAKE IT

I'm an idealist who advocates black women getting their share of the American Dream. I'm also a realist who knows that as it stands, the Dream, where the husband earns the money and the wife marries it, was not created with black folks in mind. The simple truth is that most black men aren't rich. The majority are just as hardworking as you are. They are in the same boat as you—they are just average human beings trying to make a decent living in a very unfair world.

Even the ones who have gone on to achieve higher education sometimes have to spend their lives repaying student loans. This is called being a part of the educated working poor. The reality is that there are many qualified black men who are passed over for promotions and pay increases on the job. The question is, How can you get your slice of the great American apple pie—a loving husband, a nice home, a good automobile, two or three kids, and enough money to send them to whatever schools they wish to attend and treat yourselves to nice vacations? The answer is, You can help to bake it.

PUTTING YOUR LIFE ON HOLD WAITING FOR A FANTASY MAN IS SELF-DEFEATING

In the average black household, it takes a double income to enjoy a really fine standard of living. This is a wake-up call to the sisters who are letting each day of their lives slip away, waiting to entrap a man who will pay their bills.

An example: Thirty-seven-year-old Roxanne, a production assistant, has been celibate since her thirtieth birthday. She says she is saving herself for her future "rich black husband." For the past seven years, she's been complaining that she's tired of working, saying, "I just want a rich black man to marry me and take care of me, so all I'll have to do is stay home and breast-feed some babies."

A few years ago, the prerequisites for her ideal husband were: rich, light-skinned black, handsome, tall, well-educated, well-spoken, and nice. As the years flew by and no suitor applied, the list read: rich, light or brown-skinned black, tall, handsome, and nice. The following year it read: rich, brown or dark-skinned black, and nice. The next: rich and black.

After Roxanne's thirty-seventh birthday, her list was further narrowed—to rich. After some deep deliberation, she shared, "You know, I just want a rich husband. And right now I don't care what he looks like. If he's ugly, I don't have to have a big wedding. We can go to the justice of the peace, so none of my friends will see him and laugh at me if he looks funny."

If This Isn't Desperation, Then What Is?

When she shared this, I replied, "If you have to hide someone you hope to marry, what kind of life do you think you'll have?" Our dialogue continued like this:

DR. CORNISH: Instead of wasting your years away desperately waiting for any guy who happens to have money to come along and help you to get a life, why don't you get back into the stream of life and start dating again? But look for a kind and dependable, honest, working man, and you can work on building a good life together.

ROXANNE: No way. If I can buy a leather coat on my own, why should I settle for a man who can buy me just another leather coat, instead of one who can buy me a full-length mink?

DR. CORNISH: Roxanne, having someone who cares enough about you to buy you a leather coat is better than being out in the cold alone with no one to share warmth with. You have spent seven years searching for the mink-coat man and he has not turned up yet. Why not give a leather guy a try and build from there?

ROXANNE: Who needs to struggle? I don't want any man who I have to creep through life with. I want one who has already done well for himself.

DR. CORNISH: You should choose a man who is able to hold his own, but what you are looking for is not a compatible companion, but a caretaker—any caretaker, so long as he can pay your bills. What about character? From reviewing your list, you seem to have thrown it out the window. What about your self-worth? You have actually wasted seven years of your precious life holding out for the man with the highest dollar worth, even if he happens to have the lowest self-worth.

GET OUT OF THE FANTASY AND STEP INTO REALITY

Roxanne, like so many sisters, has bought into the Cinderella fantasy. They put their lives on hold for years, waiting to be rescued by Prince Charming. Each day that the fantasy fails to materialize, sisters wrap themselves more tightly in the self-defeating blankets of celibacy, overeating, obsessive dieting, or excessive shopping. They go on shopping sprees where they will spend a dime even though they only earn a nickel at work. This gets them deeper into debt, yet they rationalize that it will be okay, for one day soon they'll meet their rich black prince who'll take care of all their bills.

Roxanne would have been better off if during the past seven years she'd attracted a nice, decent working man and they had put their two nickels together to make a dime and purchased a small but meaningful portion of the American Dream. Instead she has experienced none of the Dream at all. She is building her life upon unrealistic expectations. If Roxanne doesn't wake up soon, she'll certainly be faced with an American nightmare—a life of loneliness and unfulfilled dreams.

UNREALISTIC EXPECTATIONS LEAD TO CONFLICTS OF INTEREST

Black men and women are at odds in relationships. Sisters claim that brothers select mates based on looks only, or "how fine she is." Brothers claim that sisters choose mates based on money only, or "how much he has." Here's a dialogue that took place in one of my workshops:

LORRAINE: Black men are too cheap. They expect you to look pretty and get all dressed up, or else they won't give you a second look. They'll put their best foot forward on the first two dates, but by the third, all they want to do is take you to McDonald's and get sex, too. They want you to look good on their arm so they can show off to the world: "Hey, look what I got." Well, maintenance costs. It costs to get your hair and nails done at the salon. It costs to have the right look. Everything costs, from your dress, shoes and pantyhose, to your lotion, cosmetics, and lace panties. We are spending our money to look good for them. It's expensive. Then, when we ask them to help us out with some money, they call us gold diggers. They want to have the best without the price. I'm not having it.

MARVIN: I'm tired of hearing black women talk about how cheap black men are. It's not that we are cheap; it's just that black women are gold diggers. I can't really speak for all black men. I can only talk for me. I'm just a working man, and I can't afford all the things black women ask for. If I take a woman out to a nice restaurant, that's at least seventy dollars there, then she wants you to buy her perfume and flowers, too. They look in magazines, on television, and at the movies and daydream about what they want and expect you to fit the fantasy. I can't do it.

"AIN'T NOTHING GOING ON BUT THE RENT!"

There's nothing wrong with being pampered. Sisters should be pampered and respected. The issue here is about selling yourself to the highest bidder. By all means, first choose a good man. And if he's a provider, even better. But to settle for being misused just for money messes up both your reputation and your life. And to stoop to using a brother just for money is deplorable because it is unfair to him, too.

Here's an example from an episode of *Ricki Lake* entitled "Guess What? I'm Moving, and You Are Not Coming with Me!" Patsy, a thirty-one-year-old sister, told her live-in lover that it was eviction time. He had left his wife and had moved to another state to live with Patsy. They had been living together for over three years, and he was paying her bills. She said that she was tired of him and that he had to go because he would not file for a legal divorce from his wife. He said he would file for a divorce. She said it was too late. He was confused because he thought things had been going well between them.

An audience member told her to stop using the divorce issue as an excuse and to share the real reason why she was leaving him now, since she had known all along that he was married. Patsy responded that she had found a new man to pay her bills.

At this point Ricki asked me to share some advice. To Patsy, I said, "I'm going to give you a copy of my book *Radiant Women of Color* so you can empower yourself and select a compatible mate, so you don't have to go into relationships feeling that you have to use someone in order to pay your bills."

Ricki asked me if I would stay after the show to help the couples out. Patsy was disturbed by what I had told her, but I said she had to be realistic with herself and realize that it was precisely because she was looking for a caretaker that she had become stuck in a situation with a married live-in lover for three years. Now that she had found a substitute caretaker, she had the ammunition to replace him.

I added that if she didn't break the cycle, she'd continue to spend her life just selling herself to the highest bidder, and that one day, if she wasn't careful, she could really end up being hurt, just as she had hurt and embarrassed her lover on national TV. To him, I said, "I'm sorry to see you go through this, but I guess now you know how your wife felt when you abandoned her for another woman." He agreed.

FRIENDSHIP IS THE BEST PLACE TO START

Sisters are always complaining that there are no good men to be found. But most of these sisters have not put forth the effort to really look for a good man. On one of my appearances on the live morning show *Good Day New York,* the topic was "Where Are the Men?"

"There is no man shortage," I expressed. "It depends on what you are looking for. If you want a date in New York, you can find at least three dates per week. If you want a relationship, that's a different story. You have to first know what you are looking for."

Let me ask you this: Have you truly looked for a good partner to share with, or have you been looking for a provider to take from? It is no secret that most women are looking for a man to take care of them. I strongly believe that there is nothing wrong with wanting to be nurtured. However, we must learn to take care of ourselves and look out for a man's interests as well, so it's a healthy give-and-take.

If you want a meaningful relationship, you have to use a holistic approach—look at the person internally as opposed to physically. When you attract someone only physically, that's all you are going to get—the physical. This is what I call a surface relationship—it has no depth. You have to mate with the mind, body, and spirit to have a long-lasting and compatible love relationship. It's the law of magnetic attraction. Whatever you give off is exactly what you get back.

THE "PAID TO BE LAID" ATTITUDE WILL EVENTUALLY MAKE YOU EMOTIONALLY BANKRUPT

Here's a perfect example of this law at work: Simone was looking for the material, and Charles was blinded by the physical. Neither was looking into character; thus they ended up short-changing each other and themselves.

Thirty-two-year-old Simone was introduced to thirty-seven-year-old Charles by her cousin Faye. Faye had already briefed her with, "He isn't good-looking, but girl, he has money." Simone, a former beauty queen, was used to men's admiring looks. Charles was not the *GQ* type she was used to dating, but with her cousin's coaching ("Don't be foolish; get all you can out of him"), she decided to date him.

Charles, who owns his own import-export business, was impressed by Simone's good looks. They started dating. He wined and dined her. After each date, Simone and her cousin would get together and talk about how Simone would "turn him into putty in her hands." Faye told her cousin to start discreetly asking for gifts after the fourth date. Simone mentioned that she had classes to take; Charles paid. Then she needed help with the rent; he helped. After about fifteen weeks of steady dating, Simone was sure she had him pegged.

Charles told her that he was really falling for her, that he'd like to get more serious, and that he was thinking of marriage. Simone acted delighted. When he left her apartment that evening, she couldn't wait to call her cousin and share the news with her. They laughed and planned how Simone would get Charles to propose, accept the ring, and then break off the engagement but keep the ring. They had been on the phone for about an hour when Charles called to wish Simone pleasant dreams and to say that he was thinking of her and that he already missed her. Simone responded, "I miss you too, baby." She had a three-way phone, and when she clicked back to her cousin, she thought Charles had already hung up. However, he was still on the line.

As Simone resumed her conversation with Faye, she happily boasted, "Guess who that was?" Laughing, Faye chimed in, "He can't get enough of you. Don't forget your poor cousin here when you marry his money."

"If he wants my good looks as his trophy, he's going to have to work for this," bragged Simone. "Girl, I'm milking him like a cow!" They both laughed as they ended their conversation for the evening.

For three days, Simone didn't hear from Charles. When she called his business, his secretary said he had had to leave town for an emergency meeting.

On the fourth day, when Charles called her, she told him she had been worried about him and asked how could he let her go so long without hearing from him. He was very casual but told her that he'd make it up to her and that he had a very special evening planned. When he picked her up, she played up how much she had missed him and how happy she was to see him. He said he'd been doing a lot of thinking, presented her with a stunning four-carat diamond engagement ring, and asked if she'd marry him. She immediately screamed, "Yes!" They slept together. He left. She got on the phone with the cousin again: "Girl, I got the ring. It is gorgeous! I think I'm really starting to fall for him." Faye ended the conversation with, "Girl, money will make anybody look good after a while, even the black ugly ones."

IF YOU KEEP DISHING DIRT, ONE DAY YOU WILL ALSO GET HURT

Charles avoided Simone for about a week, then phoned and told her that he had been thinking and that he believed he had made a mistake and had rushed into the engagement. He wanted to end it. "How dare you?" screamed Simone. "You are not getting back the ring!" "Fine," said Charles, as Simone slammed down the phone.

Simone called Faye. "Can you believe this black bastard broke up with me?"

"Why?" asked Faye.

"He said it's going too fast for him. Can you believe this, with his ugly-ass self?"

"You still have the ring, right?"

"Of course! I told him he wasn't getting it back."

"What did he say?"

"Nothing. Just 'fine,' and then I slammed down the phone. What a jackass!"

"You sure he won't come back for it?"

"He's not getting it back! He can consider it a payment for all the good sex I gave him."

Even though Simone was putting up a brave front for her cousin, she was very hurt by the breakup. She couldn't figure out why Charles had broken up with her. She called, and he wouldn't return her calls. Thinking it was because of another woman, she became very jealous and actually convinced herself that she loved him. And when she thought about him not being around to keep up the lifestyle he had been giving her, she became even more determined to get him back.

She kept calling, and after three weeks he left the following stoic message on her answering machine: "Simone, there's nothing to talk about. I have already moved on."

IF YOU'RE STRONG ENOUGH TO GIVE IT, THEN BE STRONG ENOUGH TO TAKE IT

Simone called Faye for emotional support. Faye responded, "You called him first? If he didn't call you, why waste your time? He's going to think you are chasing him and he'll play hard to get. You have to learn that men are like city trains; as soon as one leaves the station, another one comes along five minutes later. You didn't fall in love with him, did you?"

"I miss him."

"You'll get over it soon. You only feel this way because he broke up with you first. You were going to leave him anyway, remember? I've been through it. It hurts when they break up with you first—especially if they are ugly. But after a while you don't take it personally; it's just part of the game. Look at it this way: You did pretty good for a four-month investment. You got your bills paid, some really nice clothes, ate at the best restaurants, and got a fabulous ring. What are you going to do with the ring?"

"I'm going to sell it and spend the money on myself. Forget the bastard."

"Now, that's what I'm talking about! Don't forget my share. About how much you think you'll get for it, anyway?"

"I don't know. It's four carats. It's worth about sixteen thousand. They'll probably offer me ten. Meet me tomorrow and we'll go sell it."

The next day at the jewelry store, Simone actually passed out when the jeweler announced, "I can offer you ninety dollars for the gold and another twenty for the cubic zirconia stone." When Simone recuperated, she and Faye stormed over to Charles's business. She attacked him and demanded an explanation for his deceit.

Charles casually responded, "This cow got tired of being milked."

You Never Know How Much It Hurts Until It's Done to You

This happened two years ago, but Simone is still experiencing shame and embarrassment from it. She told me that she would never put herself or anyone else through anything like this again. She has decided to think for herself when choosing a man—and to choose one because of who he is, not because of what he has. She and Faye have drifted apart, but last she heard, Faye was still milking men for everything she could get.

When Investing in Your Life, Take Calculated Risks, Not Idle Ones

I told Heather's story six years ago in my first book, *The Fortune of Being Yourself*. It's worth repeating here so you can see how getting stuck on the "no money, no honey" treadmill can mess up your life. Heather's example was given in the section called "How to Solve Eight Mistakes That Block True Love." It reads like this:

Heather C. is thirty-three years old. She has built her entire life around the concept of marrying a millionaire. Every action she takes is based on this dream. She has singled out a very famous and wealthy football player whom she is determined to wed. He is aware neither of her desire nor of her existence. Because he is a famous NFL player all his games and appearances are listed by the media. She uses all of her savings to buy "the right clothing" to wear and purchases front-row tickets to his games. She keeps an update on his agenda. She sometimes takes days off from her job to be present at the events he is involved in.

She is a very attractive, glamorous, and well-poised sister. Many moderately successful brothers are attracted to her and seek to date her. But because of her obsession with the famous millionaire football player, the others haven't got a chance of courting her. She has been pursuing him for nearly four years now. He has not responded to any of her calls or letters. Yet she still maintains hopes of getting his proposal. Meanwhile the other brothers are wondering why she won't date them. When I asked her reasons, she responded in a very smug and confident tone, "They are too micro; I need a macro-personality to suit my needs." I once asked her, "What is it you like about this brother?" She delightedly responded, "I like his strengths, his ability to overcome the obstacles he has been faced with. He is a winner. He is very ambitious and I want him for my husband."

"Those qualities are very good to look for in a mate," I replied, "but how can you decide to spend your life with someone you don't personally know? You have been exposed to his public image; what about his private side?"

"I feel I know him," she quickly responded. "I want to be his wife."

"Are you sure it is not his money and fame that are intriguing you?" I asked.

"No," she answered. "After four years of studying his actions, I believe I know him."

"He is famous, exceptionally wealthy, and well-liked by a lot of women," I replied. "In order to get someone's attention, you must have something special that captures their interest. Since you are so determined to be with him, what features are you going to present to hold his attention?"

"Well," she said very boldly, "I am very pretty, well-spoken, and I have a lot of class."

"As true as that may be," I responded, "there are many other pretty sisters who are after this man. A lot of them are probably well-spoken and well-brought-up, also. You know this from attending his games. You see how many sisters are obsessed with getting his attention even if it's only his autograph. People are excited by his presence." She was listening intently as I continued, "Since you have convinced yourself that this is the man you want to marry, I suggest you should have someone introduce you at his next appearance. Or approach him yourself. Or get him out of your system. Whatever the outcome, you have got to get on with your life. Your have never even had a lasting conversation with this man and you are living your life in hopes of marrying him."

"I will get together with him," she determinedly replied. "He is the right man for me. I will not settle for anything less."

Heather persevered and finally did meet the twenty-nine-year-old football millionaire. She managed to charm him for an evening. They had sex. She didn't get a dime from him. He got married to a twenty-one-year-old college graduate six months later. Heather refused to speak about the matter, and we lost contact.

BREAK THE CYCLE BEFORE THE CYCLE BREAKS YOU

After not hearing from Heather for six years, one day I bumped into her by chance at Saks Fifth Avenue. Her appearance had changed a lot. I asked how she was doing, and she responded, "Just trying to make it." I gave her my number and she began to call often for advice. Heather was still determined to marry a millionaire.

During one of our conversations, she shared that at a recent family reunion, she'd met a very nice and single forty-one-year-old black man who was an old college buddy of one of her brothers. According to her description, he had some money, was good-looking, had his own home, and was interested in dating her. "But he won't do," she added. "Why not?" I inquired.

HEATHER: He's only a teacher. He has a law degree and he's wasting it on teaching. If he wants me, he's going to have to quit that teaching job and put his law degree to better use, so he can earn more money and buy a bigger house. That little three-bedroom home won't do.

DR. CORNISH: Heather, stop and listen to yourself. Here you have a decent man interested in you. If you don't like him for his personal characteristics or mannerisms, that's one thing, but to put him down like this just because he doesn't measure up to your expected monetary standards is unreasonable and ridiculous. He's making an honest living. He's already bought his own home and he's probably very happy in his chosen profession. This is a successful black man whom many sisters would love to meet.

HEATHER: Not successful enough for me. I am not "many sisters"; I am me. I want a man who will buy me a large mansion in the suburbs, a penthouse apartment in the city, and give me a weekly shopping allowance of a thousand dollars, and he can't do it on that teaching salary.

DR. CORNISH: Heather, do you realize you sound like a gold digger?

HEATHER: *(Offended)* I am not. I admit I have lofty ambitions, and I will not settle for an average man. Everyone knows I want to marry a millionaire. If that makes me a gold digger, then so be it.

IF YOU CHOOSE SUPERFICIALLY, YOU WILL BE CHOSEN SUPERFICIALLY

DR. CORNISH: All right, Heather. Let's get realistic here: What do you have to give in exchange to capture a millionaire's heart and attention? *(This reminded me of the conversation we had had six years earlier)*

HEATHER: I am me!

DR. CORNISH: And? *(She was very annoyed at this point, but I continued)* Heather, there is nothing wrong with wanting a rich, successful, and powerful man. But you are looking for a man based on surface values only. What if the type of men you're looking for only choose women on superficial qualities also? What if they are only looking for a twenty-three-year-old, size-seven, bronzed-skinned Barbie doll clone—a trophy wife? Be real; look around you. Most forty-year-old millionaires sport twenty-year-old models on their arms. You have to be aware of what your competition out there is. How are you going to measure up?

YOU'VE GOT TO BE REAL IF YOU REALLY WANT A MAN WHO IS IDEAL

DR. CORNISH: You can always lose the weight you've put on over the years. But you're never going to be twenty years old again. Stop this. Stop wasting your life like this. You have dismissed some really decent men in the past. Don't make that mistake again. Life is a two-way street. If you go around ruling others out based on unrealistic expectations, you'll be ruled out the same way. Here you have a moderately successful man who fancies you, and you are shredding him to pieces just because he's not a lawyer? Have you ever thought that the best way to get a lawyer is to become one yourself?

HEATHER: *(Extremely angry at this point)* I don't want to talk about this anymore. I just know what I want, and that's that.

Heather closed the conversation and has not discussed the matter with me since. This reminds me of the old saying, "You can lead a horse to water, but you can't make it drink." As I said in the introduction to this book, I will provide a clear vision of the bad choices that sisters make that mess up their lives, but *you* have to be willing to face your own individual truth, so that you can fix it and create a better and more fulfilling life for yourself. A lot of us go through life with blinders on. As the saying goes, "There's no man blinder than the one who refuses to see."

INSTEAD OF GAMBLING FOOLISHLY ON A MAN'S WORTH, WHY NOT INVEST WISELY IN YOUR OWN?

Here's the point: The thousands of dollars that Heather spent on the "right outfits" and on traveling around the country trying to entrap the millionaire football player could have been invested in her own career and education. She could even have put herself through law school and *become* the lawyer she's now prowling for. And she still can and should invest in herself.

But Heather is not willing to face her truth at this point. She is very determined to stick to her goal of marrying a black millionaire. And she has a very minute chance indeed, because less than 1 percent of the entire black American population are millionaires. She's setting herself up for a big letdown. Although anything in life is possible, in this case, it just won't happen. She is betting on an opportunity where the odds are not in her favor.

Life is like a lottery—you've got to play to win. To control the luck of the draw, you must invest wisely. By investing in your own abilities, you can never lose. You lose when you vicariously put all your chips on someone else's future. When you gamble, especially with your life, take calculated risks, not idle ones. Invest wisely—invest in *you*.

STOP LOOKING FOR A MAN TO FIX YOU; START BY FIXING YOURSELF FIRST

In my personal experiences, I have been involved with both extremely wealthy men and moderately successful men. And what I've found out is, it really isn't about how much money a man makes, but the level of comfort you and he feel with each other.

I can just hear some of you sisters interjecting here: "Comfort can't pay my bills."

No, sis, but *you* can pay your bills. You created them. Take care of them. Just cut back and stop spending beyond your means.

Do you know that national surveys and statistics reflect that black women are the biggest spenders across America? It is a national joke that if all the black consumers would stop shopping for just one day, the American economy would collapse.

Let's take cosmetics as an example. Revlon estimates that black women spend over $600 million a year on cosmetics. This is at least three times the amount spent by any other ethnic group, yet blacks make up less than one-tenth of the entire American population. Isn't this frightening?

Now for shoes. Sisters and shoes: I don't personally know any black women, including myself, who doesn't own at least twenty pairs of shoes. Isn't that something—one pair of feet and at least twenty pairs of shoes? Many are the same style, in four or five different colors. The same goes for our outfits. I bet if you go into your closet right now, you will find shoes that are just collecting dust because they haven't been worn yet. Or clothes you forgot you had—many with the price tags still on. But you saw them in the store and just couldn't pass them up, rationalizing, "This would look nice on me. I'll find someplace to wear it." Every week we surrender to this voice, and we buy more and more. And when the credit card bills comes and we get frustrated, we go out and buy ourselves additional "treats" just to cheer ourselves up. Next month the bill comes again and we treat ourselves again—and so goes the cycle of our spending habits.

STOP WEARING YOUR WEALTH ON YOUR BACKS

With such careless mismanagement of funds, no wonder we go seeking a man who can pay the bills. But guess what? The brother is struggling with his own excessive-spending-to-prove-he-is-somebody identity crisis. That's what it's all about. Black people overspend because we are such harsh judges and critics of each other. We do it to impress others. We want to prove that we have "arrived," that we've made it in America.

We have convinced ourselves that when we spend $250 on a pair of designer shoes that cost only $20 to make in some factory, we are above the masses. Just as the brother who spends $200 on a pair of mass-produced name-brand sneakers that cost only $10 to make believes that he's "saying something."

Manufacturers and mass-producers of designer labels know that blacks are present-day fashion slaves. Their advertising campaigns are cleverly created to target free-spending black consumers. And it works. Because we, black men and women alike, have bought into the seduction. And in an effort to prove that we are making it in America, we strive to outdo, outdress, and outdrive our own brothers and sisters. We have been suckered into believing that by owning mass-produced designer items, we are part of the elite class. These mass-producers are laughing all the way to the bank, while you are suffering from migraines worrying about how you're going to pay this month's bills.

If you really want to make it in America, you should think smart and buy a quality, attractive pair of shoes for $50 and put the remaining $200 in the bank.

PENNY SILLY AND POUND FOOLISH IS A DIRECT ROUTE TO BANKRUPTCY

Ruby, a thirty-eight-year-old, divorced, single mother of a fourteen-year-old son, is a classic example of a sister who lives on the financial edge. Although she makes a pretty good salary as a pharmaceutical products sales manager, she is actually living from paycheck to paycheck. All of her weekly earnings come in one hand and go out the other. Her salary is spent on buying the most expensive designer clothes and accessories for herself and her son.

At first she purchased only the Izod brand for her son. When the alligator logo became stale, she purchased exclusively Ralph Lauren's Polo label. Then her son announced that he had outgrown Polo and that all the other kids in school were wearing the Tommy Hilfiger brand.

Although she was having financial difficulties, Ruby packed up all of her son's onetime favorite designer clothes, gave them away, and bought a complete new wardrobe of the Tommy Hilfiger label—from the jackets, sweaters, and shirts to the jeans, socks, and even boxer shorts. In this section I will address the strain Ruby's spending habits are causing in her personal life. To address the values she's passing on to her son would take a whole other book.

If Ruby could afford these clothes with ease, it would be no problem, but she has gotten stressed-out and sometimes even sick over worrying about how to make ends meet. In anger, Ruby admonishes, "Any man I get involved with has to be rich. Look at all the stuff I have and how rich I look. I'm sorry, but I'm not going to hook up with any man who can't maintain my lifestyle. And I don't care if anybody is wondering why I don't have a man, because I'm not going to take up a regular one just for the sake of saying I have a man."

LOOKS ARE TRULY DECEIVING

What Ruby needs to face is that *looking* rich and *being* rich are worlds apart. With the good salary she earns, if she invested it wisely, she could *be* rich. But her compulsion for material show has left her practically broke.

This is a compulsion that contributes to the aggressive and selfish behavior many sisters take into relationships. Let's get truthful here, sis: If a brother is not cruising in a luxury car, sporting designer suits, or speaking in smooth, deep tones, he's written off as nobody worth knowing. I have news for you: Some of the biggest tricksters around are the slick-looking, smooth-talking, well-dressed brothers who have developed and perfected the gift of gab.

ALL THAT GLITTERS ISN'T GOLD

Here are four flashy players who agreed to share their "programs" as long as I agreed to keep their identities secret:

GREG, 39, TELEMARKETING REPRESENTATIVE: This is my style: What I do is take her out to dinner on the first date. On the second date, I offer her sixty dollars to get her hair styled at the beauty salon. Women love that. By the third date, she gives it up. If I like her, I keep her around for a little while; if not, I move on to the next opportunity.

ERIC, 36, USED CAR SALESMAN: The type of work I do gives me access to any car on the lot. My boss and I are cool, so he lets me borrow the ride of my choice. I love to borrow the Porsches. Sisters go crazy over a black man in a Porsche. I pick up about three women each week. Usually by the first or second date, we've already done the wild thing. You'd be surprised what a sister would do for a black man in a Porsche. My, my, my. I don't keep them for long, though, because they may figure out my game. Each month, I take a week off to rest, then I just pick up where I left off.

BOBBY, 28,   Everybody uses everybody. Sisters like a lot of money.
BANK TELLER: And I like a lot of sisters. When I go to a club sporting my Armani suit, I've got it made. I only have one, but that's all you need to make the first impression. When I see the woman of my choice for the evening, I zero in, buy her a drink; she asks me what kind of work I do. All I say is, "I'm in banking with an interest in investing." Right away she assumes I'm a big-time investment banker. That seals it right there. I offer to drive her home—sometimes she tries to play hard to get. But by the time we get outside and she sees the Mercedes-Benz, Jaguar, or Lexus, which I usually lease on weekends, I strike gold—most of the time right there in the backseat. I return the car on Monday morning.

BERT, 43,   I tell them I own the limo company and that my
LIMO DRIVER: driver called out sick, so I had to substitute. I offer free limo rides. After about a week or two, I tell them I'll pay half of their rent. That does it all the time. I change about two or three women each month, just before the rent is due. All it costs me is gas money.

A Genuine Diamond Is Often Hidden in the Rough

When choosing a man, don't be misled by outward appearances. Make sure you get to know him well for who he is, not what he projects. Because all that glitters isn't gold. His inner worth could be tarnished bronze. The opposite also holds true. Some of the simplest-looking men are the truly successful ones.

In August 1996, I received a special invitation to do a discussion and book signing at the Smithsonian Institution's 150th anniversary celebration in Washington, D.C. The event was held at the Anacostia Museum. The discussion was centered on the how the relationships between black men and women will affect the future of the African-American race.

After the discussion and signing, Winston, a forty-two-year-old brother, approached me and thanked me for speaking about the average, everyday, hardworking black men who get passed over for the "pretty boys." Here's a brief portion of what he shared:

"I'm a blue-collar worker. I am an electrical technician. I wear a uniform to work. I work on the telephone poles outside. Every day sisters pass me and won't give me the time of the day. But on the weekends, or on my days off, it's a different story.

"When I'm dressed in a suit and driving along in my BMW, sisters are breaking their necks to get my attention—the same sisters who won't even glance in my direction when I have on my uniform. I own my own home, which I had specially designed and built from scratch. I am a financially comfortable man. I want a sincere mate. I want to take care of her. I can more than afford it. But I'm just tired of the games and the phony sisters who only want you after they find out what you have."

Now this is a truly good man. He's not glittery, but he's certainly worth his weight in gold. This is where the real prize is. So never judge a book by its cover—check out the various chapters within.

IF YOU TREAT A MAN AS A MONEY OBJECT, DON'T BE OFFENDED IF HE TREATS YOU AS A SEX OBJECT

When twenty-nine-year-old Petal, a part-time model, first laid eyes on Ronald, a charming and successful thirty-six-year-old national public speaker, she knew she had to have him. At the time she had a steady boyfriend of three years, Semour, a thirty-one-year-old aspiring musician.

At the end of Ronald's speech, which Petal was attending,

Petal waited until the room was practically empty, then glided over to him in her formfitting tangerine tapered suit. She knew she had his attention when he quickly answered the questions of the two people on line in front of her and rapidly ushered them off to the side.

Petal told Ronald that she was interested in becoming a spokesmodel and asked if he would be able to give her some guidance. He said he'd be delighted. He invited her for coffee, and she accepted. They exchanged phone numbers.

Ronald's career always had him on the road. He would come to Petal's city about twice a month, and they would see each other. They developed a sexual relationship. Ronald would take Petal on shopping sprees and bring her gifts. During this time Petal was still involved with Semour, who thought they had a monogamous relationship. Whenever Ronald was in town and spent the night at Petal's apartment, she would call Semour and tell him not to come over, explaining that she was revising her résumé or working on some other project pertaining to her career. She would always end the conversation by telling Semour that she loved and missed him. Ronald would witness this and comment that he hoped no woman would ever do that to him. Petal was enjoying the attention—she had not considered Semour's feelings at all. She just loved being spoiled with Ronald's gifts.

AN IDLE PROMISE IS A COMFORT TO THE GULLIBLE

Ronald had promised to buy her an apartment and told her that someday maybe they would get married. She broke off her relationship with Semour. Ronald went overseas to give a speech in Nigeria, and when he returned, he brought back three beautiful traditional African dresses in different colors. He showed her all three and told her she could choose only one.

"What do you mean, *one*?" she asked.

"One's for you. You get first choice; the other two are for two other friends."

"Friends? What kind of friends? Are you sleeping with other women?"

"Well, you didn't think you were the only one, did you?"

"Of course I did! That's why I broke it off with Semour. Because you were talking about marriage and buying me my own apartment."

"I said I was only thinking of it. Baby, be real; after the way you treated that brother, telling him you loved him, laughing at him while making it with me in the bed, I could never trust that you wouldn't do the same to me."

Petal became angry. Ronald stood his ground. They argued. He left. He didn't called for weeks. During that time she called his answering machine at least three times every day. She called him everything from a "coward" to a "bastard."

One day he finally called her machine and left this message: "Baby, do us both a favor—just give it a rest."

Petal ended her story with the following declaration: "You know what? I'm just really very mad at black men right now."

WHY PUT A PRICE TAG ON YOUR EMOTIONS?

Sisters like Petal are motivated by greed. They become weakened by money. They'll quickly trade sex in hopes of having their bills paid. A woman like this will use her body to entrap a man in exchange for money. As time goes on, she may come to believe she is falling in love with him. Then, when the brother does not return the emotional feelings she expects, she is devastated!

Can one clutch fire to her bosom and not be burnt? The man in this situation will usually leave as soon as a more interesting "sex object" comes along, just as Petal had left Semour as soon as Ronald, the "money object," came along.

The physical and material aspects of relationships, without the mental and spiritual bonding, are shallow and will never last. Sisters who measure the worth of a brother by the car he drives, the position he holds, or the clothes he wears, without consideration of the feelings he has, are shortchanging themselves.

It is definitely important to look for an ambitious companion who has the drive to do well in life, but to choose or refuse a brother based on what he has or what he doesn't have, and then get upset when he does the same thing to you, is downright ridiculous.

Isn't It Time to End the Masquerade?

Black men and women play such unnecessary games with each other. We claim we don't understand each other, but we are actually more alike than we are different. If we would only let our masks down and take the effort to really get to know each other as friends first instead of viewing each other as "objects," we would genuinely like each other.

But everyone is afraid of taking the first step, so we continue on this malicious seesaw trip, keeping ourselves up while pressing others down. It's that "burn them before they burn me" attitude, with the sisters declaring, "I'm milking him like a cow," and the brothers jiving, "Why buy the cow when I can get the milk for free?"

Is this what we've come to: Reducing ourselves and each other to the level of cows? After all these years of struggling together for freedom in America, we are now struggling against each other for power in the bedroom?

Go figure!

bad choice

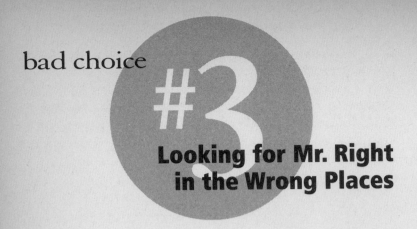

#3

Looking for Mr. Right in the Wrong Places

The second quality on a sister's list of what she seeks in a man is status.

Take this test: Tell any of your girlfriends you've met a new man. The first question you'll be asked is, "Does he have money?" followed by, "What does he do?" There will be further inquiries as to the initials, if any, attached to his name, such as Ph.D., M.D., C.E.O., and M.B.A. The more prestigious the initials, the more you will seem to be validated in their eyes. This suspicion will be confirmed by the high-pitched squeal, "Go on, girl, you did well."

Without even a breather, you'll hear, "How does he look?" "Is he tall, short, light-skinned, dark-skinned; does he have a good body?" Then, "Does he drive?" If you answer yes to all of the above, the next series of questions is, "What kind of car does he drive, what make, what model, what year?" Somewhere at the end of the conversation, the friends may remember to ask you, "Is he nice?" and "How does he treat you?"

Sociological studies support the theory that while black men choose women by their degree of attractiveness, black women choose men by their degree of status. There is a gulf between black men and women, a vicious relationship battle that has gotten out of hand, due to miscommunication.

Instead of Waiting for the M.B.A. Start Looking for the J.O.Y.

Do you know how many sisters I encounter who have their lives in a state of suspended animation waiting for a black man with a title to come along? Many of these sisters have kept themselves on hold for four years or more. Many are denying themselves the joy of experiencing compatible relationships with decent black men, all because of the lack of a certain level of status.

Some of the loneliest and most unhappy sisters I know are the ones who adamantly refuse to date any black man without a certain level of wealth or status or a high-powered job. An astonishingly high percentage of sisters would rather be alone or cross the color line than have a relationship with a black man "below their level."

Here's an example in one of the letters I published in my advice column in the *New York Beacon*:

> Dear Dr. Cornish:
>
> I have been celibate for five years. I am 35, very attractive, professional, and financially secure. I would like to meet the right man and get married. The problem is I'm having the hardest time finding a decent, eligible Black man.
>
> I'm an executive at a major computer company. I've worked very hard to reach where I am, and I refuse to date below my level. The type of Black man I want always seems to be taken, and I don't believe in man-sharing.
>
> I'm not particularly attracted to white men, but that's all I am surrounded by at work. Two have recently asked me out. I've never thought of dating one before, but now I'm wondering if I should give it a try. What should I do?
>
> H. T., Manhattan

The Best Place to Start Is to Look into His Heart

Dear H. T.,

Your dilemma is not an isolated case. Many upwardly mobile Black women are faced with the dilemma of either man-sharing, becoming "born-again virgins," or dating men outside our race. Statistics tell us there is a Black man shortage, but this is not the root of the problem.

The problem is that many sisters are looking for "Mr. Right" in the *wrong places*. Many are by-passing eligible, caring, respectable blue collar Black men for the limited pool of executive or doctor types.

As far as not dating a man below your "level," you are right. No one should get involved with anyone they are not compatible with. However, what is your "level" based on? Is it only the size of his billfold, the position he holds, or the car he drives? A genuine level of compatibility is found in a man's heart and not in the double-breasted suit he wears. A decent man is not necessarily the one who makes six figures, but the one who will share his innermost thoughts, dreams and fears with you, regardless of the type of work he does.

As far as your dating a white man, that's a personal choice which is entirely up to you. However, you seem to be entertaining this idea as a desperate outlet. Desperation is no reason to date anyone. If you decide to date a white man, do so because you really like him for the individual he is and not because of a falsely assumed Black man shortage. What you need to do is look within and identify what is truly important in a mate.

Your Prince Charming may be wearing a blue collar uniform. Stop limiting yourself; you may be missing out on the love of a lifetime. Compatible love is sharing, caring and kind.

THE EMPTINESS IN YOUR LIFE CANNOT BE FILLED BY THE EMPTY PROMISE OF SOMEONE ELSE'S STATUS

Many sisters who have made it professionally are scouting for a C.E.O., M.D., Ph.D., or M.B.A. as a complementary partner. And that's understandable. They have had to pull their own weight and make a lot of sacrifices to get where they are. Although there is no shortage of good and eligible black men, the reality is that professional black women far outnumber professional black men. Unfortunately, the long and lonely journey has left many black women feeling hardened against and resentful of the black men who have not made it. These sisters will admonish, "If I could do it, why can't he?" The joke is that many of the blue-collar black men the sisters are refusing earn twice as much as some of the white-collars they are pursuing. What's equally unfortunate is that a percentage of black men who have become successful professionally have convinced themselves that they can never find equal success with their female counterparts and have chosen to cross the color line instead.

IT'S A DISGRACE TO BELITTLE YOUR OWN RACE

Now, I personally have nothing against interracial relationships. It's a personal preference, and black men and women alike should enjoy loving whomever they choose. But for any brother or sister to say they "had to" choose elsewhere, because there are no good or eligible partners in their own race, is both shallow and blind.

This is from thirty-three-year-old Mia, a beauty editor, who recently married a white partner: "I've dated many successful black men. They always treated me like a trophy. Most of them are too pretentious and stuck-up. The ones with the M.B.A.s wear their degrees like medals around their necks. They always wanted to show me off because I am light-skinned, but they were never emotionally available. I have had too many bad experiences with them. They cheat too much. I just got tired of black men and I decided I would never date another one. And then two years later, I met my husband, who is white, and he loves, supports, and respects me."

If you fall in love with a person of another race, you shouldn't have to explain or make an excuse to anyone about your choice. It's actually no one's business. Love is love; enjoy it. But do yourself and all of us a favor, please: Do not put down your very own black counterparts by uttering belittling and insulting remarks such as "There just aren't any good ones left."

A Higher Degree Does Not Guarantee a High Degree of Character

This is where many sisters trip themselves on life's path. They believe that getting involved with a brother with educational accomplishments and degrees behind his name guarantees living "happily ever after." This is not so. A degree, a job promotion, an expense account, or an attaché case does not substitute for character. Character is a person's inner worth. It is what determines the state of relationships. Good character contributes to a successful union; lack of it leads to a failed affair. A man's external standing can be worth millions while his internal worth is zero. If he has nothing substantial within, believe me, he cannot enrich your life in any way.

You should always strive for upward mobility. It is nice to have a black man who is ambitious enough and disciplined enough to have lifted himself to a higher standing in society. If you happen to have a healthy relationship with a decent brother of this standing, that is fantastic. But the belief that social status automatically guarantees a loving relationship is erroneous.

PRETENDING TO BE SOMEONE YOU AREN'T IS NOT A HEALTHY WAY TO GET A RELATIONSHIP

Many sisters will stifle their true personalities in order to entrap a man for his title. The problem with this is that if you are so busy trying to get the guy to like you, you aren't going to stop to see if you truly like him.

Karen, a thirty-two-year-old black receptionist, wants very much to be married to a black man of high social standing. She met Terrance, a thirty-four-year-old successful black financial planner, at an annual black M.B.A. networking party. She was there as a volunteer for the company sponsoring the event. They were attracted to each other. Terrance asked her out, and she accepted. They went out the following week.

Karen was always taught by her mother, "Get yourself a successful black man. Marry someone who has made something of himself. Don't end up with a nobody. Successful men like women who support their interests and ideas above everything else."

Karen wanted Terrance to like her enough to eventually propose to her, so on their date, she acted in a way that she thought he would appreciate. Although she disagreed with some of the things Terrance said, she wouldn't let him know it. Black women are often stigmatized as being aggressive, and she didn't want him to think of her in that manner. She thought it would scare him away if she appeared to disagree with his ideas. In short, she pretended to be someone she wasn't. Karen, usually a vibrant and talkative sister, didn't say much throughout the date, but she smiled a lot. At the end of the date, Terrance told her he would like to see her again. She thought to herself, "Terrance likes me this way. He is a good catch. I don't want to lose him. I have to show him I agree with his ideas."

After eleven months of deferring to Terrance and still receiving no proposal, Karen realized that her own feelings were being neglected. She became dissatisfied. She could no longer keep up the game she had begun. She needed to express her own wants and could no longer put him in first place. This, of course, took the brother by surprise. Terrance had gotten comfortable in this position. He refused to relinquish his lead in the relationship or to compromise. Both were hurt and disappointed; they seemed to have become incompatible, and all they had left in common were their conflicts. They drifted apart. The relationship ended with both of them being miserable, unhappy, and bitter.

THE TRUTH WILL ALWAYS SET YOU FREE

The emotional tragedy of Karen's relationship could have been avoided if honesty had been present from the outset. Either she and Terrance would have gotten together based on mutual respect for each other's interests, ideas, and feelings, or they would have decided that they were not compatible and avoided the pain of a failed relationship.

Karen was dishonest with both herself and Terrance. She denied herself by playing a role she assumed he would like, all because she falsely believed her true nature wasn't good enough for his M.B.A. status. She denied the brother by not giving him the opportunity to know the real Karen.

Karen was misguided by her mother's advice. Her mother meant well, but Karen couldn't be happy acting differently only to please her man. Eventually the disharmony had to manifest itself. Shakespeare said it best: "To thine own self be true. Thou canst not then be false to any man."

TRADING SEX FOR A TASTE OF STATUS IS BOUND TO WRECK YOUR LIFE

Karen was not being fair to herself—she was selling herself short. What's surprising is the extent to which some sisters will go just to be with a famous or high-powered man. Many compromise their self-worth and self-respect just to be in such a man's company.

A very good and platonic male friend of mine, who is a famous and successful best-selling author and businessman, is one of the most sought-after black bachelors because of his status. We ran into each other in Chicago at the annual American Booksellers Association convention, where we were both scheduled for a book signing on the same morning. We hadn't seen each other since the previous year's convention. When he came over to greet me he looked exhausted, and I jokingly told him that he looked like a wreck. He laughed and said, "I know, Doc; it's because of having too many women. I need help. Analyze me."

Then he became serious as he shared the following story: "You know, Grace, women complain that men are wild, but you don't realize exactly how wild women are. Every city I go to there are women, all kinds of women, who initiate sex. Sometimes I get so exhausted, I just fall asleep, and they lay right there in the hotel room. After a while it just becomes routine. But last night this one really got to me. I had a dinner meeting with a public-relations representative in the hotel restaurant. She was gorgeous. The type of woman that would make a man think he had died and gone to heaven. I had planned to take it slow with her; get to know her better and possibly get into a relationship. After we had drinks she invited herself up to my room. As soon as we got into the room, she pulled my pants down and performed oral sex. I really did not expect this. I asked her why. Then she looked at me in surprise and said, 'Don't you know who you are? You are the famous [his name].' Man, this one really disappointed me. I could never respect her after this."

He was in no way sharing the incident in an egotistical tone. He was actually baffled that the sister so freely traded sex for status. But trying to keep a compassionate psychological balance, I responded, "It takes two. If you can't respect her, I guess you can't respect yourself, either. If you call her a slut, then that makes you a male slut. It doesn't make you a Casanova, like you would love to believe; it just makes you a male slut—maybe a famous and wealthy one, but nonetheless, you're still one anyway." At this point, he laughed and said, "There you go again, Doc, always defending your sisters."

NO ONE'S FAME IS WORTH THE PRICE OF YOUR SELF-WORTH

But even though my friend's own behavior was questionable on many levels, he was right to be shocked by that sister's behavior. How disgusting and self-defeating of her to get so personal with this man she didn't even know. He could have had a lethal disease; she didn't care. She was just too caught up in his fame. No one's fame is worth the price of your self-worth! Sis, stop cheapening yourself. Most men won't refuse sex. They'll get caught up in the moment and take it for what it's worth. But if you expect to get a respectful relationship afterward—forget about it! They will grab your goods and run like a thief in the night, and then label you a "slut" on top of it. But this is the price you pay when you give up sex too soon. We will talk more about that when we discuss Bad Choice #4, "Exchanging 'Sexual Dealings' for Loving Feelings."

Many sisters mistakenly believe that sleeping with a famous or wealthy man validates them. Many wear their sexual conquests like badges of honor. A sister who sleeps around with "average" men is considered loose, but a sister who sleeps with a famous or wealthy man is considered special in her clique. She gains a false sense of identity through association with his image. How truly sad. Lord help the sister if the infamous mister should ever fall from grace.

INSTEAD OF GOING AFTER SOMEONE ELSE FOR HIS ACCOMPLISHMENTS, WHY NOT CREATE YOUR OWN?

Instead of putting a man on a pedestal because he has achieved a certain social status or because of his educational accomplishments, invest in yourself. Put your time and energy into becoming the best you can possibly be in this lifetime. The secret to success in any endeavor is built upon two things: purpose and discipline. Know exactly what you want and discipline yourself to achieve it—one step at a time. That's exactly how our ancestors built the wondrous pyramids, one stone at a time. It's human nature to be fascinated by what we think we cannot have. It becomes a mystery. A close friend of mine once shared, "What we are attracted to in other people is what we long to become ourselves." If you accomplish your own level of success, then you won't have to ransom your self-worth to taste someone else's.

CHOOSE BEFORE YOU LOSE

June, a thirty-eight-year-old legal secretary, has been celibate for two years. She has made a promise to herself that she will get married only to an exceptionally successful black man. One of June's coworkers told June that her cousin is an assistant district attorney who is single and available and who makes a decent living. She said she would arrange for them to meet. Instead of accepting the invitation to see if they would be compatible, June's question to her coworker was, "Do you think he is ambitious enough to become a judge someday?" Her coworker took offense and introduced her cousin to another sister, whom he is now dating. June is still alone and celibate. Need I explain why?

SEE BEYOND HIS ACHIEVEMENTS AND LOOK INTO HIS HEART

Linking up with a brother of high social standing doesn't come with a guarantee of instant happiness. Don't get misled by this fantasy. All relationships take work. They take patience. And sis, believe me, what it boils down to is, a man is a man. The additional initials after his name do not promise that your relationship will be any more enjoyable or carefree. So please stop putting your life on hold for that fantasy.

As a matter of fact, many sisters complain that a lot of upscale, successful, middle-class black men know that they are viewed as ideal prospects and use their status to sample various women. On a personal note, I find that this may only apply to brothers with a nouveau riche mentality who are still trying to get comfortable with their newly acquired success. The well-bred successful black men are very kind, sincere, and decent. They are so comfortable with themselves that they have no need to impress anyone or put on false airs. They make some of the best mates and companions a sister could ask for.

AVOID THE TRAP OF A NARCISSISTIC CHAP

The following brother is certainly not one of the good guys:

Thirty-nine-year-old Lawrence has an M.B.A. and owns a very successful real-estate business. He has been engaged three times in the past and is currently in the process of ending a two-year relationship with Paulette, with whom he shares a six-month-old baby. He has given Paulette a house but has told her that he needs his freedom. She's devastated and heartbroken. He cannot understand why she is "giving him grief," since he's leaving her with a house. Maybe one day Lawrence will be mature enough to understand the meaning of the popular song by Luther Vandross: "A house is not a home when there is no one there to hold you tight, and no one there to kiss good night" . . . especially when you're left alone with a new baby. Lawrence candidly shared, "I don't believe I can ever settle down with one woman. I haven't met the one good enough for me to marry yet."

Lawrence is a commitment-phobic and narcissistic brother who suffers from confusion. He is standing on his own pedestal, tooting his own horn about how "good enough" he is. He is not looking for a companion; he's looking for a cheerleader to cheer him on and worship his overinflated ego. Paulette should have seen the red flags from his previous three broken engagements. Lawrence is going through life afraid of making a commitment because he is afraid that a more suitable mate will come along. A lot of sisters are going to travel on his heartbreaking brick road before he ever gets around to choosing one. Hopefully they'll detect the warning signals of this indecisive, egotistical, dysfunctional brother and avoid being blinded by his status.

"LET'S TALK ABOUT WHERE WE'RE HEADING BEFORE WE GET TO THE BEDDING, BABY"

The following is another letter from the *New York Beacon,* this one from a sister involved with a commitment-phobic psychotherapist:

> Dear Dr. Cornish:
>
> I have been dating the same man for the past two years. We have many common interests and goals. He is a 42-year-old psychotherapist and I am a 36-year-old guidance counselor. Neither of us has ever married. Our relationship is fun and comforting. He enjoys spending time with me and has taken me on many mini-vacations. He lives in Connecticut, and I live in Manhattan. We speak to each other every day on the phone and spend practically every weekend together.
>
> At the beginning of our relationship, he said he didn't want a commitment, but as the months passed, we both agreed to have the AIDS test and, after negative results, we have been having unprotected sex.
>
> We have met each other's families and we go to church together almost every Sunday. I have shared everything with him, including the keys to my apartment. I also believed he did the same, until three weeks ago.
>
> I was feeling really happy about being in love and wanted to show him how much I cared. I decided to cook him a special meal and surprise him in the middle of the week. I took the food to his home unannounced. Well, I

was the one who was surprised. Although he invited me in, he told me never to visit without prior warning again. He said he could have been entertaining a guest and that it would have been awkward and embarrassing for both of us. I felt as if he had driven a knife through my heart.

Although he didn't confirm it in words, his actions led me to believe we had been having a committed relationship. I find it impossible to be at ease with him since then. I am upset and unhappy. In order to be physically intimate with him now, I have to have a glass of wine to drown out the sorrow I am experiencing. Should I continue seeing him or am I wasting my time being loyal to someone whose actions say "yes," but [whose] words say "no?"

J. M., Manhattan, NY

No Monogamous Contract, No Sexual Contact

Dear J. M.:

There is an old saying that "actions speak louder than words"; however, in this case another proverb takes precedent. "By a man's words you will know the deeds of his heart."

I strongly suggest that your psychotherapist be psychoanalyzed as to why his psychological behavior is so foreign to his physical and emotional behavior. His body is giving you one message, while his mind is speaking a completely different language. This is a commitment-phobic man who is either consciously or subconsciously toying with your emotions. He ought to know better, especially given the nature of his profession. How dare he agree to have unprotected sex with you, knowing that he may be "entertaining" others? He has you in a state of uncertainty, where he can easily say "I told you so." If he insists on being "only friends," then stop sharing your privacy with him. Friend-

LOOKING FOR MR. RIGHT IN THE WRONG PLACES

ship should not cross the boundaries into romance unless both parties have a compatible agreement to respect each other as lovers.

First of all, take back the keys to your apartment. Secondly, do not under any circumstance use alcohol to pacify the hurt you feel from this man's behavior. This can lead to an addiction. Do not mess up your life for anyone. Third, be completely honest about your feelings. Don't hold back, or pretend or force yourself to feel comfortable with him. If it doesn't come naturally and he's not willing to work with you in regaining trust, there's only one thing to do—dump him!

CHOOSE A MAN BECAUSE YOU <u>WANT</u> HIM TO LOVE YOU, NOT BECAUSE YOU <u>NEED</u> HIM TO EMPOWER YOU

Selecting a mate to share your life with is a very special decision. It should be done with great care. In order to maintain a pleasing relationship, you must first be pleased with who *you* are. Don't ever turn your life over completely to anyone. Many sisters get involved in order to fill emptiness in their lives. The brother becomes a need, especially a brother with status attached. What these sisters are actually saying when they declare premature love for this type of man is, "I need you and your title to make me feel lovable and valuable. If people see that I have a man with a degree, then that will make me a more respectable black woman."

If you don't view another person's status as a means to filling your own needs, then you won't be devastated by his failure to do so. Choose a brother because you like him for who he is. *Want* to be with him, as a likable individual human being. Don't *need* to be with him for the initials he has accumulated behind his name. Wanting to be with someone is a healthy choice. Needing to be with him is a dependence. Too much dependence on anything or anyone eventually becomes destructive.

Don't Get Fooled by the Fantasy

Twenty-eight-year-old postal worker Candice experienced the danger in choosing someone for status only. She had been dating Gary, a fellow postal worker, for seven months. The relationship was going along fairly well until she suspected he was having an affair with another coworker. She confronted him. He denied it. She didn't believe him. They argued, and she decided to go out for drinks that Friday evening with some of her single girlfriends.

Her girlfriend Pat remarked, "Let's go get some upscale men and give these tired post-office brothers a rest." The sister-friends all dressed to the nines and decided to visit a trendy, upscale buppie restaurant-bar in Manhattan. The Friday evening after-work crowd was very lively. At first everyone seemed a bit standoffish, forming little three- and four-person clusters. But as the evening progressed, and after a few drinks had been downed, brothers and sisters started to mingle more freely, leaving the "home bases" they had established.

Candice's girlfriend Pat discreetly elbowed her in the side and said, "Girl, check out that chocolate Adonis checking you out!" Candice turned in the direction her friend suggested, and her eyes locked with those of one of the most handsome, well-dressed black men she had ever seen. She tried to hide her admiration by sipping her drink, but spilled the drink as he started to walk in her direction. He wore an elegant charcoal business suit, a crisp white shirt, a deep emerald-green silk tie with a navy-blue Cartier links print, and a pair of bottle-green Bally shoes.

"Hello, beautiful, I'm Brian. May I buy you another drink?" A bit nervous, she accepted. She shared her name and they exchanged stories for the next three hours. She told him she worked in the post office; he told her he was an M.B.A. and a partner in a marketing firm. He told her he had no business cards on him, so they handwrote phone numbers.

They started dating. She eventually found out that Gary's infidelity was only a rumor, but she told him it was over anyway. She joked with Pat, "Why should I go back to beer when I now have champagne?"

CLOTHES DON'T MAKE THE MAN; BE ALERT AND CHECK OUT HIS INNER WORTH

Candice had been with Brian for three weeks. During that time, they dined out twice per week. He told her he got paid monthly and asked her to cover the bills until the end of the month. He promised he would reimburse her, plus take her away on a weekend trip. She believed him. She asked him for his number at work. He told her the company's name, but told her his position was so demanding that he couldn't be disturbed. Two days later, she had a burning curiosity to call him at work. She got the number from directory assistance. She dialed and asked the receptionist for his extension—only to receive a puzzled "Who?" She repeated his name. This time the response was, "I'm sorry, we don't have anyone here by that name."

Candice was completely confused. She consulted Pat. Pat advised her not to confront Brian yet, but to play detective first. After three days of discreetly staking out his house and following him around, they found his true place of work and his position—he was a stock clerk at a department store. The fancy clothes he wore had been purchased with his employee discount. When she confronted him face to face, he wasn't even ashamed of his lies. He threw his hands up in the air and said, "I didn't force you into anything. You wanted a fantasy and I gave it to you."

LOW-QUALITY CHAMPAGNE WILL ALWAYS GIVE YOU A HANGOVER

Candice was swindled by this calculating con artist who pretended to be the upscale man she was seeking. This trickster could probably sell ice to Eskimos, but Candice should not have been taken in by his appearance. Many of these con artists will even go so far as to purchase a new attaché case to complete the look of success. And if you ever got a peek inside, you would find nothing but a brown-bag lunch and a banana for dessert. Sisters, check out the man's credentials thoroughly before getting involved!

Candice had all the early warning signals to get out of this situation from the beginning. The moment he started asking her for money, a "jerk detector" signal should have gone off. But she was so busy buying into his story that she was blinded to the blatant truth that stared her in the face. It is men like these who give the truly decent brothers a bad rap. Brian had an honest-paying job as a stock clerk, but he used dishonesty to swindle free meals out of this anxious sister. She gave up a guy who didn't cheat on her for one who actually cheated her—all because she was deluded by "champagne" illusions.

STOP SELLING YOURSELF SHORT

I met Carmen at one of my book signings at a writer's conference. At the time she was a freelance editor who had worked for various black magazines. After the discussion and signing, she introduced herself to me and asked if she could interview me for a story. We scheduled the meeting for the following week. After the interview, she told me that she was celibate and asked my advice about the best places to meet nice and successful black men. I shared my list of the top ten best places, but added that the best thing for her to do was to either get friends to introduce her or to go places where she was genuinely interested in being. Then if she did meet a man, they would likely have some hobbies in common.

Carmen would call from time to time to let me know how her search was coming along. I hadn't heard from her for about five months, when one day she called to ask for some advice. She shared that she had been hired as a sportswriter for a major black radio station. During this time, she'd made some good friends. There was one brother, Marc, she was particularly interested in. He was in the publicity department. She had asked a mutual friend of theirs at work to introduce them. He had, and they had found each other mutually attractive. He had asked her out, and she had accepted. On the first date, after the movies, she had invited him back to her apartment, where they'd played strip poker. He'd won. She'd stripped. He'd spent the night. Over the next two weeks, he'd spent practically every night at her apartment.

LOOKING FOR LOVE THROUGH STRIP POKER? YOU MAY GET ONLY QUICK SEX AND A JOKER

The last Saturday night they spent together, he said, "I'll see you at work on Monday." When she went to work on Monday, he was not there. She thought he was sick. She called his apartment. No answer. She asked the friend who had introduced them if he knew where Marc was. He said no. Over the next few days, she neither saw nor heard from him. During this time she was getting more upset and worried. She was wondering if something serious had happened to him. After a week and a half, she couldn't take it any more and again approached the mutual friend and pleaded with him to level with her. His reply was unexpected. He related that he had told Marc to level with her from the beginning, but that Marc had refused to. He said that Marc had gotten a job promotion and moved to Detroit and had told him not to give Carmen his phone number. She said she didn't believe him. He dialed Marc's number in Detroit on the speakerphone, so she could hear his answering machine. Carmen was deeply hurt.

"How could someone just disappear without any kind of warning when things seemed to be going so well?" she wanted to know.

"People do some strange things. You can never account for anyone's behavior. That's why you must always protect yourself and get to know someone well before taking him into your heart," I responded.

A Jerk Is a Jerk, Regardless of His Work

"I would never have expected that from him," she sighed. "I thought he had more class and consideration than that. Because he is an educated black man, and because of the position he had at work, I felt comfortable with him. I let my guard down. I shouldn't have, should I?"

"I think you already know the answer to that one. His position at work has nothing to do with his position in relationships. You gave yourself too readily, and he enjoyed the moment. He is a creep for disappearing without even having the decency to bring closure to your affair. I agree he should have been more thoughtful of your feelings, but this is not about him. It's about you taking care of yourself so you won't get fooled like this again."

"This makes you lose faith in black men," she claimed. "Makes you almost want to see a white guy."

Don't Bash the Whole Bunch Because You Bit a Bad Apple

"You know, Carmen," I said, "if I had a dime for every black woman who has said that to me this year alone, I would be rich. I'll tell you this: If you repeat the same mistake and play strip poker and sleep with a white guy on the first date, then we'll be having this conversation again, but the next time you may be declaring that you want to see a Chinese guy instead. You have to take responsibility for your actions. Changing a man's race won't solve the problem, but changing the way you allow men to treat you will. Next time go slowly, and look into the guy's character and relationship background instead of his position at work."

CAN THE NEED TO IMPRESS OTHERS COMFORT YOU WHEN YOU ARE ALONE AT NIGHT?

Two years ago, thirty-six-year-old Elaine, a certified public accountant, contacted me because she was having difficulty deciding if she should marry a man who was not in her professional bracket. She was afraid of the opinions of her family and friends. She shared that she had experienced many unfulfilling relationships in the past and had not dated anyone for two and a half years until she had met James, whom she'd been secretly dating for one year. She said he cherished and adored her, and she was "falling in love with him." He had asked her to marry him. She admitted that she kept him hidden from her family and friends. I asked her why.

ELAINE: He is only a security guard.

DR. CORNISH: Why is his work a problem? He's making an honest living, isn't he?

ELAINE: Yes. But I always believed I'd marry a doctor or a lawyer. My family expects it. What will my girlfriends think?

DR. CORNISH: You have to define what *you* really want in a mate and what you can honestly give in return. You are ashamed of openly loving a man whose company you enjoy and who makes you feel good about yourself, all because of wanting to impress others.

ELAINE: They are going to think I got desperate and settled. They're going to think I could do better.

DR. CORNISH: Elaine, you have been alone for so long. You've met someone who brings you joy. Allow yourself to be happy. Can your family's and girlfriends' expectations comfort you when you are alone? Can their opinions fill your loneliness?

ELAINE: No, they can't. But it is such a hard decision.

WAKING UP JUST A LITTLE TOO LATE

Elaine was still so caught up in what her friends and family would think about James's status that she kept postponing and stalling until one day he finally confronted her—and she admitted to him that she was embarrassed that he didn't have a higher standing in life. He was hurt. He left and never called her again. She missed him, but her false pride wouldn't let her call him. About four months later, she realized she had made a big mistake. She called his home and work, and found out he had moved from both. She had no means of contacting him. She is still hurting today. Here's the part that drove Elaine back to see me: One of her professional girlfriends from whom she was hiding James is now happily married to a doorman from her previous apartment building. What a lesson!

INSTEAD OF WORRYING ABOUT WHAT OTHER PEOPLE THINK, THINK ABOUT WHAT'S BEST FOR YOU

Too many sisters live their lives by worrying about how others view them. They wonder, "What will other people think?" This is a very self-limiting attitude. They allow this fear to control their lives. It destroys their spontaneity, creativity, and curiosity. It prevents them from getting the love they want, having the kind of fun they want to have, and doing the things they want to do.

During every phase of their love lives, they ponder, "If I date him, what will my family think? How will it make me look?" This becomes the deciding factor in their choice of dates. They are reluctant to date someone without high social standing, for fear of being laughed at or not being accepted. So they do what they think others will accept and they neglect their own desires. All too often this leaves them depressed, bitter, and lonely.

YOUR LIFE IS NOT A DRESS REHEARSAL; THIS IS THE REAL THING, SIS!

Life is too short to be wasted wondering about what others think. We live our lives sandwiched between two pieces of paper—a birth certificate when we enter and a death certificate when we exit. The time in between is a beautiful, precious gift from God. Enjoy it. If you meet a decent man who loves, respects, and appreciates the unique individual you are, then share your journey with him. And if others refuse to understand or approve of your choice, let that be their problem, not yours.

Instead of being fearful of others' opinions, each sister should be concerned about her own love life. Ask yourself, "What is truly important to me in an ideal mate? And why?" Don't limit yourself by locking yourself behind a certain status barrier. Venture out and meet brothers of different caliber.

Florence, a forty-year-old executive for a four-star hotel chain, said she is very happy in her twelve-year marriage to Joseph, her forty-four-year-old carpenter husband. This is how this white-collar sister met her blue-collar partner:

They met fourteen years ago when Florence first started out in the hotel business. She was a floor supervisor, and Joseph was repairing one of the suites on her floor. Whenever she stopped by the suite to inspect the repair, he would flirt with her. She thought he was charming, but never took him seriously because as she put it, "He just wasn't my type. When he first asked me out I looked him up and down and thought, 'He can't be for real.' He was sweaty from the construction work. I turned him down. But he wouldn't give up. He asked me out to dinner every day for three weeks straight, and he was nice about it, so I finally said yes.

"When he cleaned up for our date, he looked really good," she said, blushing. "We talked and shared a lot with each other. After our first kiss, I knew he was the one for me. Ten months after, we were engaged; two years after, married. We saved together and bought our dream home. And after all these years, and two beautiful kids," concluded Florence, "he's still my Mr. Right. He's my best friend."

IF YOU WANT A MR. RIGHT, YOU HAVE TO BECOME A MS. RIGHT

One of the most common mistakes we make is neglecting to take stock of our personal assets and liabilities and make a true summary of what we can offer a mate in a relationship. A healthy relationship has to be balanced. While you are looking for Mr. Right, he is also looking for Ms. Right.

Nobody can become the right mate for you until you become right with yourself. Take a true look at your life, and be honest: Have you done the best with your talents? Are you feeling good about the things you are able to control at this moment—your grooming, your finances, your personality? Are you willing to truly work with a mate and go the distance, or are you hoping that he'll answer all your dreams? Are you willing to be supportive of his interests also? And here's the most important and difficult one to answer: What is unique about you that will make you the right mate for him? Set some time aside and really take stock of yourself and write ten good qualities that you have that can bring joy to someone else's life.

When you are finished, give yourself credit for it. Next, write ten things about yourself that you want to improve. Notice I didn't use the word "change." Don't ever try to *change* yourself for anyone, but always strive to *improve* yourself and your qualities. You can change your outlook, but not your essence. After you list your ten points, make a commitment to *you,* to better yourself. Start now with the things you can improve right away. Realistically, it's not going to happen overnight, so give yourself a time period to commit to bringing out the Ms. Right in you.

IF MR. RIGHT WAS STANDING IN FRONT OF YOU, HOW CAN YOU RECOGNIZE HIM IF YOU HAVE BLINDERS ON?

Before you inquire about *where* to look for Mr. Right, you must first ask *what* to look for *in* Mr. Right. As we can see from the stories shared here, money and status do not create the ideal mister, although they certainly would be good frosting on the Bundt cake, so to speak. But the cake must first be baked with character.

The purpose here is to show you not to be blinded by status, but to choose wisely by character, regardless of the man's station in life. Whether he is the executive who runs the boardroom or the maintenance man who cleans the boardroom, you must look first at his character and how he treats you.

THE "S" FORMULA FOR CHOOSING MR. RIGHT

Make sure he is:

1. *Supportive* He appreciates your worth and wants the best for you. He encourages you to follow your dreams and ideas.
2. *Smart* He is an intelligent and creative thinker. He is sensible and self-aware.
3. *Successful* He has his own job and he does it well. Whatever position he holds, he makes an honest living and keeps himself out of debt.
4. *Sweet* He is kind, compassionate, and considerate of your feelings. He respects you and really cares about your well-being.
5. *Stable* He is dependable and loyal. He is not a womanizer. You don't have to worry about him being fickle or cheating.
6. *Stimulating* He is a good conversationalist. He keeps you mentally interested and challenged. He likes to learn and share new things with you about life. He isn't boring.
7. *Sensitive* He is emotionally open with you. He's strong enough to share his fears and his feelings with you. He's not afraid to cry in front of you.

8. *Single* He is available. He is not already in a relationship with another. He believes in monogamous unions.

9. *Straight* He is not a closet bisexual or homosexual man. He is a truly heterosexual male.

10. *Sensuous* He is romantic, charming, and sexy. He is appealing and has excellent hygiene. He is clean and smells good. He cares about pleasing you—from head to toe.

If you settle for anything less, you will be making a poor choice. If you are in it for the long haul, choose wisely. But make sure you are the female version of what you are looking for in a mate. You too must be the right sister for the right mister.

THE TOP TEN PLACES TO MEET MR. RIGHT

I conducted a national survey of two hundred and forty happily married couples and newlyweds and asked them for the best places to meet the right partner. They shared the following as the top ten:

1. Work
2. Homes and parties of mutual friends
3. Special-interest classes
4. Conferences and conventions
5. Concerts
6. Social and community events and activities
7. Church
8. Public transportation—train stations, bus stops, airport terminals
9. Libraries and bookstores
10. Weddings

Don't Choose Him Because of Social Pressures; Don't Refuse Him Because of Social Stereotypes

The best way to meet an ideal mate is to get out of the house. The wrong place to look for Mr. Right is in front of your TV set—you won't meet him sitting at home alone, tying yourself to the tube, and eating ice cream for comfort. You won't meet him by hanging around with a bunch of your lonely girlfriends complaining about how bad black men are. You will meet him if you get up, get out, and get going. But you must choose wisely. This is especially true for the sisters who have been alone for a while. Don't just pick a man because of social pressures, and don't disregard a decent one because of social stereotypes. Don't be fooled like some of the sisters in the stories I've shared with you.

Although traditional wisdom advises that church is the best place to meet a respectable and nice man, there are some factors to keep in mind. Since all single sisters know this, the churches are filled with twice as many single women as single men. So it's best to keep church as your sacred place to worship and pray and not to go there for the sole purpose of meeting a man. However, if you do meet him there, then so be it.

If You Want to Meet a Businessman, Then Go Where Businessmen Congregate

Some of the hottest places to meet available upscale black men are the black business conventions. There are conventions for black professionals in various fields—from bankers, dentists, and psychologists to journalists, attorneys, and government officials. There are thousands of eligible black men who attend these annual conventions. However, be aware that many sisters have complained that some of the well-dressed, Armani-suited executive brothers display egos even larger than their cell-phone bills. Anyway, one sister's *mistake* may be another sister's *beefsteak*. If you decide to give the convention route a try, you can find out more details by contacting your local convention center or chamber of commerce, or by reading trade journals of the fields you're interested in and talking to people working in those fields.

Wherever you decide to look, keep in mind that seeking a union based solely on a title instead of looking for a soul mate messes up your life. Judge a man by his inner worth, not by his outer initials.

THE DIFFERENCE BETWEEN MR. RIGHT AND MR. WRONG

Mr. Right is:		Mr. Wrong is:	
M	Mature	**M**	Manipulative
R	Respectful	**R**	Ridiculous
R	Real	**W**	Womanizing
I	Interesting	**R**	Raunchy
G	Generous	**O**	Obnoxious
H	Honest	**N**	Narcissistic
T	Trustworthy	**G**	Gloomy

WHY PUT YOURSELF THROUGH THIS?

Last summer, Denise, thirty, contacted me, very confused as to whether she should continue to see her forty-year-old lover of four months. She explained that he refused to have a monogamous relationship with her. He was currently seeing two other sisters, and whenever they came into town, Denise was not allowed to see him.

"Why don't you just leave him? What's the confusion?" I asked.

"He's a doctor. I don't want to give him up," she whimpered.

"If this same man was a mechanic, would you let him use and disrespect you like this?"

"No way. I would drop him immediately," she replied.

"Then why degrade yourself just because of someone's status?" I had to ask.

If you are putting your life on hold and desperately seeking validation through a brother's status, you are messing up your life. Think about it. Do you think the man would really respect you if he sensed you only wanted him for the initials attached to his name? Why sell yourself short? Always go for the J.O.Y. before the C.E.O.

bad choice

#4

Exchanging "Sexual Dealings" for Loving Feelings

We have all heard the saying "haste makes waste," but all too often we fail to apply this logic to the act of sex in our relationships.

Too often sisters surrender sex too soon, without a compatible agreement, secretly hoping that somewhere along the way the man will eventually fall in love with them. And when he fails to make a deeper commitment, or when he pulls a disappearing act, we get hurt.

We get hurt because we fool ourselves into believing that if a man enjoys having sex with us, enjoys breathing hard and enjoys coming back for repeated performances, then it must mean he is in love with us. Nothing could be further from the truth. What he is in love with is the performance, not the performer. He may appreciate you for sharing the act with him, but in his mind appreciation does not equal commitment. That's why it's up to the woman not to give sex so quickly and freely if she has any intention of having a fully committed relationship and not just a sexual one.

Now don't feel that I'm out of step with "the modern-day sista," or that I'm telling you to put your sexual life on hold and become celibate. I am not suggesting that sisters become born-again virgins. However, I am suggesting that for your own emotional protection, you should reach an understanding before you engage in sex, so that you will know your partner's intentions and won't be caught off guard if he suddenly becomes the invisible man.

Is a Night of Passion Worth the Follow-Up of Pain?

This is how Sonya set herself up: She believed there was something more substantial to her sexual fling than there actually was. She met Calvin at a victory celebration party for the election of their city's first black mayor. She had played an active role in the campaign and was a key presence on the mayor's platform. Calvin was a reporter covering the event. He interviewed her about the mayor's intentions regarding the inner-city crime rate. She had experienced a bad breakup in a previous relationship and had not dated for three years. She found Calvin attractive, and she told him so. He was flattered and asked for her phone number.

They spoke frequently during the following week, and he asked her out to dinner. During dinner they talked about their individual career plans and goals. She enjoyed his company, and he told her he was impressed with her. She didn't hear from him for two weeks, but then he called and asked her out again. During dinner he told her he was attracted to her, but he wanted to take things slowly because he was still getting over a recent breakup.

Over the following months they spoke only periodically on the phone. Sonya had spent the past three Valentine's Days single and alone, and she didn't want to do so again this year. With all the Valentine's Day hype, she was feeling lonely and wanted to be in someone's arms. Because of her attraction for Calvin, she called him at work and asked if he would come and spend Valentine's Day evening with her. He was flattered and excitedly asked, "Are you serious?" She said yes. He brought a bottle of wine. They shared a Valentine's toast. They had sex. The following day he called and they spoke briefly. After that, she didn't hear from him for three weeks. She was hurt, but she called him anyhow and disregarded her true feelings.

IF YOU KNOW THE BURNER IS HOT, WHY KEEP TOUCHING THE STOVE?

During their conversation, Sonya told Calvin she wanted to be with him again and asked if he would come over. He said that he had injured his knee in a skiing accident two weeks prior and was on crutches, but that he would come over to have sex with her. He wobbled over to her apartment, still in pain from his injury, and jokingly said, "The things a brother would do for sex." They had sex. He left right after. She thought that because he came over in pain, "just to see her," that meant he found her special. However, she didn't hear from him for another six weeks. She was even more hurt, but again she called him, and again she buried her true feelings. She pretended all was well and told him she had just called to say hello. He told her that he hadn't called because the last night he had gone to her apartment, someone had broken into his car. He was very casual and nonchalant and made no attempt to see her.

She shared with me, "I'm so hurt. I can't believe he could be so cold to me after we shared such intimacy. I'm confused and I don't know what to do. I'm really hurt because I feel he took me for granted."

GET THE AFFECTION BEFORE THE ERECTION

Now show me a sister who cannot identify with Sonya's deep hurt, pain, and embarrassment. Remember this song: "Will you still love me tomorrow?" In our deep need to be cherished, we tend to fantasize and mistake the act of sex for the feeling of love. We just blindly jump into the pool and hope we won't drown, without first taking any necessary safety precautions.

When I followed up by asking Sonya her feelings about having sex with Calvin before discussing their relationship with him, she shared, "I just wanted to feel loved. And then when he ignored me, I felt used. I really feel ashamed that I just gave myself to him like that. I've honestly never done this before, but I just got tired of being lonely. And he was available, and he seemed so real. I really grew to like him. And I thought that since he had sex with me a second time, that he actually liked me too."

ACTIONS SPEAK LOUDER THAN WORDS; IF HIS ACTIONS SAY HE DOESN'T WANT A RELATIONSHIP, BELIEVE IT!

Sonya left herself wide open to being used because she failed to have a complete discussion with Calvin before they had sex. She should not in any way blame him for her choice to offer him sex. He told her he wasn't ready for a relationship. She was lonely and she wanted comforting, and that's understandable, but she incorrectly assumed that their having sex meant something deeper for Calvin. This happens quite often to sisters, especially if they've been lonely for a while. We tend to overromanticize and fantasize about sex.

KNOW THE REAL FACT BEFORE YOU ACT

Never assume that you know what someone else is thinking. Before you engage in sex, talk about where it's leading. I'm not advocating that you remain celibate, but don't just share yourself with anyone without first getting to know the type of person he is and what his true intentions are. This will prevent a lot of misunderstandings and hurt. Ask him directly what he's looking for. If he tells you he doesn't want a relationship, believe him. As in Sonya and Calvin's case, he may have recently broken up with a former mate and he may be emotionally unavailable.

We are frequently misled by our own wishful thinking instead of looking at the actual facts. We falsely convince ourselves that what the person tells us isn't true. In our minds, we mold the man into the character we want him to become, because we are sidetracked by our own unfulfilled needs.

You must listen carefully and respect his decision. And you must ask yourself if this is all you really want. If you are convinced that you can handle a sex-only relationship, then make sure you can keep your emotions out of it and will not switch in midstream when you want it to mature into something more. A sexual relationship is just a sexual relationship. Nothing more, nothing less. It may last for several years, but if you don't share a deeper level of commitment, it will remain purely sexual.

A ROSE BY ANY OTHER NAME IS STILL A ROSE; SEX BY ANY OTHER HOPE IS STILL JUST SEX

When Julie first met Walter she had already been involved with her boyfriend, Howard, for two years. She had asked Howard to marry her, but he had said he wasn't ready. She was annoyed and started having a sexual relationship with Walter. She enjoyed sex with Walter. She continued seeing Howard during this time, but was progressively growing less sexually attracted to him and more intensely sexually attached to Walter.

Three and a half years later, Howard finally asked her to marry him. This time she told him she was not ready to marry him. Then she called me to ask what she should do about her predicament.

DR. CORNISH: Why are you dating two men at the same time?

JULIE: Well, Howard is almost perfect. He is there for me and truly cares about my feelings. I know he truly loves me. I feel comfortable with him, but I don't enjoy him sexually. He's more like a friend. But Walter excites me sexually. He's perfect in bed. But he's made it very clear that he is comfortable being single and he's not about to go deeper than what we have sexually.

DR. CORNISH: So let me understand this: You are using one for security and the other for sex?

JULIE: Yeah. I guess so.

DR. CORNISH: Why?

JULIE: I just wish I could take certain pieces from the two of them and combine them into one man.

DR. CORNISH: Which man?

JULIE: I'm not really sure. But I wish I could put Howard's attentiveness and love for me into Walter and have him marry me.

DR. CORNISH: Have who marry you?

JULIE: Walter.

DR. CORNISH: Why?

JULIE: Because I love being with him.

DR. CORNISH: What about Howard?

JULIE: He bores me. I like him as a friend, but I hate when he touches me sexually. Every time we have sex, I close my eyes and pretend it's with Walter instead. But I know he will always be there for me. Whereas Walter has told me ours is only a sex relationship, I guess I'm holding on hoping Walter will change.

DR. CORNISH: It seems to me you have already made up your mind which one you want to marry. First of all, it's unfair of you to keep Howard dangling on a string if you don't really love the guy. He sounds like a really nice man, and he deserves to be free so he can find someone who truly loves him for who he is. You are already cheating on him now, and you'll continue to cheat on him if you get married. So why bother? What kind of marriage would that be? As far as Walter, you are agonizing over him now, but you knew the relationship was only sexual from the beginning, and you allowed it to grow as such. So why do you think you're going to change him now? You are being unrealistic. And the longer you keep on this sexual roller coaster, the more you are going to hurt yourself and Howard.

JULIE: You're right. I should let Howard go so he can be with someone who loves him . . . but I don't think I can be without Walter right now. I'm going to wait and see what happens.

DR. CORNISH: That's your choice, but trust me on this, Julie: If a man tells you he doesn't want a relationship beyond sex, it means exactly that. Believe him; he's a grown man. He knows what he wants. Why continue to confuse and hurt yourself like this?

IF IT DOESN'T FIT, DON'T FORCE IT!

"Oh, what tangled webs we weave"; that's why we are so easily deceived. Let's take a reality check here. Since sisters love to shop for shoes, let me use that as an analogy. The dating-and-mating process is just like shoe shopping. If you get involved with a brother who isn't a proper fit—even if you think he'll eventually stretch to suit your needs—you are inviting discomfort and pain.

Unrealistic expectations and incompatibility are two of the major causes of pain and breakups. Stop trying to make men over. Many sisters go into relationship believing they can "cure" the man of his failure to commit. When this doesn't happen, they blame the guys for their disappointment or deem themselves unacceptable. It isn't that they are unacceptable—what's unacceptable is the fit. If he tells you no, it's just no. Don't force it. Don't waste your time trying to change or "stretch" him. Instead, conserve your energy and self-respect for a mature and willing man who really wants to be with you. Why subject yourself to the pain of ill-fitting shoes? Give up the torture—get a comfortable pair!

KEEP YOUR EYES OPEN FOR THE CASANOVA ON THE PROWL

As we all know, it is no secret that there are some brothers out there who live by the "Mac Daddy Hound-Dogg Code": "Feed da fantasy; tell 'em what they wanna hear." It does frequently happen that a sister may share a thorough discussion with a brother about a relationship, and think that he is on the level, but in time the truth is revealed and she finds out that he is a liar whose only intention was to make a "booty call." But let's get honest: The world has always had many of those careless chocolate Casanovas who go on the prowl, wolfing sisters every chance they get. And I'm sorry to say it always will. But my main concern at the moment is for you to take full responsibility for the choices you make and not set yourself up just to be let down. It is painful to let go of bad choices, but believe me, it is not as painful as going through years of misery with a mismatched mate.

I No Longer Enjoy This Relationship, but I Continue Because the Brother Is So Fine

Thirty-three-year-old Shana is a teacher. She is a very attractive, dynamic, and creative sister. Although she is an open-minded sister who advocates change in every area of her life from entertainment to education, she is unusually reluctant to accept change in her personal life.

Shana has been involved with Devon for a little over six years now. Devon is a thirty-six-year-old karate instructor. He is exceptionally handsome and very charming, with a dazzling smile to complete the package.

During the first two years of their relationship, Shana was deeply in love with Devon. More than anything else, she wanted to marry him. But whenever she brought the subject up, he made it quite clear, in a very polite manner, that although he loved her very much, he had no intention of ever marrying her.

Shana, who always seemed to be a self-assured sister, lost her self-esteem because of Devon's nonchalant attitude toward the idea of marrying her. Still, she continued seeing him, hoping that one day he would change his mind. Because of Devon's cover-boy good looks, sisters and women of all races always found him attractive and flirted with him. This enraged Shana. She was always fearful of losing him. She realized her emotions were unhealthy and attempted to break off the relationship many times, but they always gravitated back to each other.

Shana always dreamed of being "married with children" before reaching age thirty. She comes from a family that strongly encourages this practice. She has always felt silently pressured by this. Every six months or so over the past six years, she's tried to convince herself that she should leave Devon for good. She has always believed the wisdom handed down from her grandmother through her mother: "If a black man doesn't ask you to marry him within the first six months of courting, he has no plans to do so at all."

Shana subconsciously noted this six-month mark. When their semiannual anniversary came around, she would get angry at Devon for not proposing to her. She would break the relationship off. After a few weeks Devon would call to tell her how much he missed, loved, and needed her. She would always accept him back.

IF YOU GIVE AN ULTIMATUM, YOU'VE GOT TO STICK TO IT TO BE TAKEN SERIOUSLY

During this past year, Shana decided she had to permanently remove Devon from her focus if she wanted to move ahead. She came to talk to me about this.

SHANA: I know I'm holding myself back waiting for a commitment from Devon. Every time I break off the relationship, he comes back. I don't want to lose him, but I'm hurting myself by not progressing. Last year I convinced myself I wanted to have his child. One reason is because I'm getting older. Another is that our child would always be a reminder of how much I loved him. So even if he was no longer in my life, I would still have a part of him. Because he is so gorgeous, I am sure I would have a good-looking baby. I have not gotten pregnant yet. I realize I don't love him anymore, but I still allow him back into my life.

DR. CORNISH: Why do you keep doing this to yourself?

SHANA: I don't know. I guess it has become a habit to see him. I think I'm more in love with the idea of being in love than I am actually in love with Devon. I'm really just tired of the same thing after all these years. But the sex is still good. That's about all we have left. And besides, there are so many jerks and diseases, and there's such a shortage of black men out there, I don't want to take the chance of investing in another man.

DR. CORNISH: It seems you have given up on yourself. And you're only in this relationship for the sake of being in a relationship, with no regard for whether it is productive for either of you. You are apparently no longer in love with Devon. So are you still involved with him only because you are lonely or afraid of being alone?

GO FOR THE HEART AND NOT JUST THE BODY PART

"You know, I have thought about that many times," she answered. After a short pause she continued, "I am going to try to be as honest as I can about this. Although I am not afraid of being alone, I'm afraid of feeling lonely. I don't want to be a statistic—another lonely black woman without a man. I want to know someone loves me. It makes me feel worthy, knowing I am capable of being loved." She took another brief pause, then added, "I also ask myself, if any other man had put me through these changes, would I still be with him? The answer is 'no.'"

"Then I ask myself, 'What is it about Devon I am so attached to?' I thought about this very long and hard," she confessed. "I didn't want to admit it to myself, but I am deeply drawn to him because he is so gorgeous and because we have terrific sex. As shallow as this may sound, it is the truth. I wouldn't accept this at first, but had he been a regular-looking brother, not to mention ugly, we wouldn't have gotten past the first six months, let alone years. Every time I get angry with him, when I look at him and realize how handsome he is, for some reason I let him get away with things no one else could." She sounded very defeated at this point and looked very upset.

SHALLOW REASONS GET SHALLOW RESULTS

DR. CORNISH: Shana, you are deciding with your hormones instead of your heart. Do you feel secure with your own looks? Are you using him to boost your appearance?

SHANA: *(Brief pause)* I've never really thought about it that way. People always tell me how beautiful I am.

DR. CORNISH: But do *you* feel you are beautiful?

SHANA: Somewhat. Not as pretty as I would like to be, but better-looking than most women.

DR. CORNISH: Does being with Devon make you feel prettier? Does it make you feel more valuable for some reason?

SHANA: Actually, it makes me feel just the opposite. I feel his looks are better than mine. Although mine are fine on their own, I feel I'm overshadowed by his. But if I'm with him, I believe people will think I must be beautiful to be able to get such a handsome man.

DR. CORNISH: Is this substantial enough to base a thing as impor-tant as a relationship on? Are someone else's looks more important than your own feelings? Shana, what is it that you are holding back? Let it out . . .

WE STILL HAVE A WAY TO GO . . .

Shana was astonished by her own revelations at this point. Tears began to stream down her face. With further probing, she broke down and shared that Devon was a "light-skinned black man with green eyes" and she felt "special" that with all the women who wanted to be with him, he had chosen to be with her, "a dark-skinned black woman." She said all the black men with her complexion never looked her way and would always choose lighter-skinned sisters. Shana shared that she never felt love from darker-skinned brothers, and the only time she ever felt truly loved was when she was "making love" with Devon. She added that being involved with him gave her a sense of "victory" because Devon always took her to the best places and walked proudly with her on his arm. She said that for the first time in her life she felt like the "trophy."

DR. CORNISH: Shana, this discrimination within the black race is a shame—a crying shame. So many lives are messed up by some of the intraracial prejudices. It's truly sad that in these modern times this "dark skin/light skin" thing is even an issue. But your relationship is unhealthy because you are keeping this man on because of his looks and sex. Is this more important than your self-respect?

SHANA: He truly is a nice guy. I sincerely do like him, but I have fallen out of love with him. I feel I have wasted six years trying to get him to marry me. I can't believe I've invested all this time. I guess it's time to cut the cord. It's going to hard, though . . .

DR. CORNISH: You need to get in touch with your feelings. Take a few months away from the relationship to define what's important to you as an individual. This time, no sex with Devon until you find out for sure exactly where you are heading. Get in sync with your own thoughts, your own looks, and your own feelings. If after that you decide you want to go back to Devon, it's your choice whether or not to do so. But to be perfectly blunt with you, Shana after six years, you need to tell Devon "No wedding, no bedding." And this time, stick to it!

"LOOK BEFORE YOU LEAP"; THE HIDDEN WOUNDS MAY JUST BE TOO DEEP

Another frequent mistake many sisters make is to hopelessly confuse the act of sex with the emotion of love. There is a world of difference between "making love" and "having sex." The former is experienced when a man and woman mate in love and tenderness involving mind, body, and soul. The latter is mating for purely physical enjoyment.

Tanisha and Carl met at a party held by some mutual friends. They immediately became physically attracted to each other. As the evening progressed, the attraction grew stronger. Carl asked Tanisha to accompany him to his apartment. She accepted willingly. They had sex. Tanisha enjoyed this so much, she was convinced that it was love the first time around.

She wanted to see more of him and hoped he felt the same way. He did. They decided to see each other on a steady basis. They physically enjoyed each other very much, and Tanisha was convinced she was in love with Carl. However, as the months passed, she began to learn more about him. She began to realize their differences in their thinking. He was skeptical; she was judgmental. He was a pessimist; she was an optimist. He believed the world was against him; she believed you just have to look for the good in humanity. Other than their physical ecstasy, they had little in common.

Carl's views and opinions began to drain her energies. He was very negative in his beliefs. She spent most of their time together trying to cheer him up, to see the positive side of things. They agreed that they both faced similar racial challenges in society, but she tried to get him to focus on what he already had, instead of being down about what he didn't have. He began to criticize her for her way of thinking. Spending time with Carl, she was unhappy more often than not. But because she enjoyed having sex with him, she continued to believe she was in love with him. This is called the body-over-mind relationship.

SAY "NO" TO SYMPATHY SEX

Deep inside, Tanisha realizes that Carl isn't right for her. But she doesn't want to hurt his feelings. He suffers from depression and has lost many relationships in the past over it. She is a very compassionate and sympathetic sister. However, she is not being kind to herself. Carl has formed a dependence on her in order to nurture his own bitterness and depression. She has given in to it. She has become a "prisoner of love." Locked into a relationship dictated by her physical will, she gives little respect to her mental and emotional wills.

Tanisha attended one of my workshops. She shared that she was "very miserable" in the situation, but she enjoyed "the way Carl made love." I told her it couldn't be love, since she insists that she is so miserable. And the only way they could have a satisfying relationship would be if Carl got professional help to deal with his troublesome case of depression.

"I've tried getting him to seek counseling before," she shared, "but he says he doesn't have a problem. And if I can't hang, then he'll get someone else who understands him."

At this point, I asked, "Well, do you feel you can remain in a relationship—actually, Tanisha, I'm not going to call what you have a relationship. Because in a relationship, both people relate with each other and look out for each other's best interest. What you have is an arrangement, where you have arranged to trade your peace of mind for sex. Do you feel you can remain in this situation as it is since he says he doesn't need help?"

"Honestly, I know that being with him is really not good for me. But I would miss the sex."

Tanisha left it at that. Hopefully she'll gain enough self-respect to end this unhealthy situation, for both Carl's sake and her own. What she is doing is *sexual social work*. She is attempting to heal Carl by sacrificing herself. Her reward is the sympathy sex.

Tanisha doesn't realize that she is not helping Carl's situation by sleeping with him, pretending all is well. Nor is she helping herself by settling for only the physical pleasure in a relationship. Good sex is a vital part of a relationship, but it is not enough in itself to sustain a happy one.

A rewarding relationship consists of the mating of the mind, body, and spirit. Hopefully Tanisha will realize that she is too valuable to settle for only one-third of the joy.

Mathematics 101: Sexual Motion Does Not Equal Loving Devotion

One of the most sympathy-provoking cases I have seen of a young sister taken in by the "I'll give you sex if you'll give me comfort," trade-off was that of twenty-five-year-old Rochelle.

Rochelle suffered from low self-esteem. She felt uncomfortable with her looks. She was picked on a lot as a child, and she developed into a shy and withdrawn young adult. She never had a steady boyfriend and always dressed conservatively. At the age of nineteen, she went to her first club with one of her girlfriends from her neighborhood. No one asked her to dance. She noticed that the girls who were getting the attention were the ones who were skimpily dressed, with the most cleavage showing.

The following week, she went again with her friend, but this time she dressed very provocatively. It worked. That evening, she had a few suitors and many drinks. The evening ended with her having a one-night stand with the guitar player from the band. She enjoyed the attention. She decided she liked musicians. From then on she starting frequenting clubs with live acts, two and three times each week. Her clothing, or lack of it, got more and more revealing. As she put it, "The less I wore, the more attention I got." The evening always ended with her having sex with one or more of the musicians.

She enjoyed the attention the guys were paying her in exchange for the sex she was giving them. She decided to become a band promoter. In this way, she said, she would have access to many more musicians. She became addicted to this lifestyle.

LIVING LIKE A DOORKNOB: WHOEVER KNOCKS GETS A TURN

Rochelle worked part-time as a typesetter in a printing firm while she was building her career as a band promoter. I had the fliers for my workshops done by her company. On a few occasions, I went in to personally proofread the materials before having them printed. Rochelle would share bits and pieces of her life story with me and ask for some quick advice.

The last conversation we had was a week before Thanksgiving. Rochelle declared with a sense of pride, "These guys make me feel good. I only live once. I'm having fun and I've already made up my mind; I'm not going to change for anybody."

"Rochelle, no one can change you, but you. That is something you have to want to do for yourself. But for your own safety, you have got to tone your antics down. What you are doing is dangerous. You are playing a deadly sexual game of Russian roulette with your life."

"You don't understand; I've never had this attention before. I know it's just for the sex. But I enjoy it. Most of the time the guys don't talk to me after. But I always meet new ones anyway. I'm going to die someday anyway; I may as well go out enjoying it."

Seven months later, Rochelle telephoned to say she had been diagnosed with herpes. I cried for her. And I still do.

YOU CAN NEVER CHANGE THE OLD BUT YOU CAN ALWAYS BETTER THE NEW

Rochelle's sexual promiscuity was rooted in a poor self-image caused by childhood trauma. Early childhood experiences, or failed relationships along life's path, have left many sisters harboring self-hatred. And as an escape, many confuse trading sex for being loved. You cannot undo what was done yesterday, but you can break the pattern and create a better today. Put a high value on yourself. You are too important to give away your sexuality for nothing. The trade-off should be real love—not imagined love. Real love from a decent and deserving man who wants to be with you as part of a team. A man who gives a damn about you—one who is in your corner.

"To every thing there is a season, and a time to every pur-pose . . . A time to embrace, and a time to refrain from embrac-ing." Let's make this a time to be kind to yourself. These commitments can help:

THE TEN COMMITMENTS: "A TIME TO BE KIND TO ME"

1. A time to stop beating myself up about my past life and past mistakes. A time to say I've made mistakes—and so what? A time to move forward.

2. A time to stop condemning myself—to stop criticizing and belittling myself. A time to stop feeling insecure and bitter about what I don't have and to start counting my blessings for what I do have.

3. A time to groom myself properly. A time to make myself as healthy, clean, and pretty as I can with what God has given me.

4. A time to be truthful with my thoughts. A time to be bold and not afraid of speaking my mind or showing my true feelings.

5. A time to stop letting others take me for granted. A time to stop giving away my talents for free. A time to appreciate my cre-ativity.

6. A time to appreciate the beautiful skin that God has blessed me with, even though others may fail to do so. A time to know that I am a lovely gift from God.

7. A time to know I am worthy of love. A time to let only a nice, decent man into my life. A time to know that my sexuality

is valuable. A time to know that I'm important—and allow myself to love and be loved.

8. A time to get rid of negative energies. A time to have only good friends who genuinely care about my well-being. A time to remove all the deadweight from my life.

9. A time to say, "To hell with what others may think of me." A time to make me into what I think I should be. A time to commit to becoming the best I can be.

10. A time to just smile and welcome joy into my life. A time to just be kind to me.

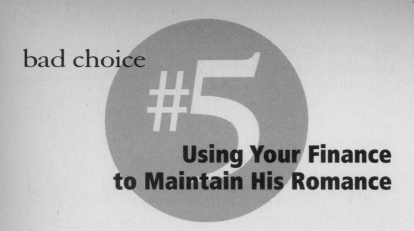

bad choice #5

Using Your Finance to Maintain His Romance

You cannot imagine the number of times I have sat and listened to sisters cry with excruciating pain over being taken for granted after supporting an estranged lover financially. I have seen first-hand results of sisters walking around with broken hearts because of giving too much and not getting enough in return. In anguish these sisters have reflected, "I don't understand what went wrong. I gave him everything I had. How could he have walked out on me after I took such good care of him?"

Twenty-six-year-old Jasmine shares, "Some of these black men love to call black women 'gold diggers,' but a lot of them are out there doing much worse. Instead of getting a regular job, a lot of them use women to pay their bills and to give them allowances."

What saddens me, and often upsets and frustrates me in these cases, is that the sisters feel that they have to *earn* a man's love by buying it. They do not believe they are capable or worthy of being loved simply because of *who* they are, so they attempt to get the man's love by *what* they can give—in this case it's their hard-earned money.

WHEN PRINCE CHARMING TURNS OUT TO BE PRINCE HARMING

Diane telephoned me with her story of the incredible dilemma she found herself in two years ago. She was still trying to find answers to what went wrong in her relationship. Here is how her story began:

Diane, a publicity events coordinator, had met Trevor at a music seminar seven years before. Although he had a stable job with a government agency, he wanted to pursue a career as a musician. She said she found him exceptionally charming and sexy, and the moment she laid eyes on him, she knew she had to have him. At the time, he was twenty-six and she was thirty-four, but his being eight years younger was not an obstacle to her. So she pursued him and set out to win him over. She told him she would handle all of the promotion for his music. She bought all the materials necessary to start a business from home—a new computer, a laser printer, a fax machine, and a photocopier.

After four short months of dating, she convinced him to give up his apartment and move in with her so they could save money by splitting the cost of rent. The money saved would be put into his music. He moved in. He quit his day job to dedicate himself full-time to his music. She kept her day job but worked tirelessly in the evenings and on weekends to build a "name" for Trevor in the industry.

During this time, Diane began to discover flaws in Trevor's personality—he would talk down to her and belittle her in public. But he would quickly apologize and he always told her it was because he felt pressured about his career. She was hurt, but she always forgave him. It became a pattern; the more he disrespected her, the more she mothered and forgave him.

IF HE IS BEING "KEPT," HE WILL EVENTUALLY LEAVE YOU IN DEBT

After a year of living together, Trevor told Diane he wanted to relieve some of the stress she was experiencing from working so hard. He said he would handle their bookkeeping and banking activities. She agreed to take from her weekly paycheck only what she needed for personal necessities, and she handed over the balance to him to take care of the bills and their savings.

Six months later, Trevor's verbal abuse intensified. He went as far as telling her that she was old and washed up, and a failure in promotion, and that no other man would want her. Then, as usual, he apologized; she accepted his apology. This went on for four and a half years of living together. One Wednesday morning in the middle of May, Trevor told Diane he was leaving her. She was devastated and begged him to stay. By the following Saturday morning, he was packed and ready when the moving company came to move him out. He gave her no forwarding address or phone number to contact him with.

BEWARE OF THE SWEETHEART SABOTAGE

At first Diane was sick with despair. Her despair turned into disbelief and anger when she received an eviction notice from her landlord and a host of lawsuit threats from collection bureaus. After looking into the chaos, she found out that Trevor had not been paying the bills, but had only paid a minimum requirement once every few months to keep from going to court. However, for the last five months, he hadn't paid any bills at all. He had also cleaned out their joint savings account. She was penniless, heartbroken, and being sued on top of it. The apartment lease, credit cards, phone, and utilities were all in her name. Her credit rating was completely destroyed.

And if that wasn't enough, here's the kicker—after running a background check on Trevor through a detective friend, Diane found out he looked like a prince on paper. His credit was squeaky clean, and he had just bought a new home with another woman, who was living with him. She could not afford an attorney, so she contacted legal aid. She was told there was nothing she could legally do to him because all the money she had given him from her weekly earnings was in cash, and there was no paper trail.

Diane got Trevor's address from her detective friend and went to confront him. He called the police. When they arrived, he told them that Diane was just very bitter because their relationship hadn't worked out. He lied and told the police that she was insanely jealous and that he believed she might be dangerous to him and his new fiancée. The cops ordered Diane to leave his property, and Trevor got an order of protection against her.

WE HOLD ON TO LOUSY RELATIONSHIPS BECAUSE WE DON'T THINK WE DESERVE BETTER

After Diane shared her ordeal with me, she asked for some advice and words of comfort. What I told her applies to many sisters: "Diane, you were trying so hard to make Trevor happy, that you were too busy to ask yourself if Diane was happy. You completely disregarded yourself. What you now have to look into is why you didn't think enough of yourself to make sure you were being treated fairly.

"When we think something is wrong with us, that's when we grab on to people in fear. We stay in lousy relationships because we believe, consciously or subconsciously, that we don't deserve any better. We feel unworthy, so we stick with 'the evil we know.' We allow our own fears to blind us, or we allow the manipulative mate to run and ruin our lives. We are convinced that this is the best we can do and that we are lucky the person is with us. This is the real failure—the self-condemning thoughts we harbor about ourselves.

"Life is not easy. We will always have a challenge. Where we get into trouble is when we expect our lives to be carefree—problem-free and happy all the time. Then when it isn't, we beat ourselves up, thinking something is wrong with us. There is nothing wrong with you. Everybody has difficulties in life. No one has a perfect, carefree life—whether rich or poor, black or white. We tend to believe the grass is always greener on the other side. We always believe others are having a better life than we are. We falsely *overestimate* other people's value, while we sadly *underestimate* our own worth.

"What you can do is develop a peaceful state of mind, so you can deal with the challenges when they do arise. And there will be many. This will help you to find effective solutions to overcome life's problems. If you are stressed-out and worried, you cannot think straight. However, if you take even ten minutes and completely block out all the external cares, you'll be surprised at the clever and creative solutions your mind will supply to you.

"I read somewhere once that life is a journey, not a destination. One of the most damaging negative energies that disrupts our journey is fear. When we are fearful of losing a person's validation, we become desperate and will do almost anything for them not to abandon us."

DON'T GET SNAGGED BY AN "ALL SHOW AND NO DOUGH" BRO

Thirty-two-year-old Lori is an aspiring singer who has been supporting her husband, thirty-four-year-old Tony, for three years. She is a strikingly beautiful sister; he is a moderately handsome Greek who is also an aspiring musician.

They met at a dance club three and a half years ago. He was still living at home with his parents. She was living in a spacious loft apartment in Manhattan. Lori has always worked between acting jobs to support herself. For the past five years, she has held steady employment as a dancer at one of the trendiest nightclubs in Manhattan. She takes home an average of six hundred dollars per night and works three nights per week. When she met Tony he was unemployed. They found each other attractive and started dating. Lori paid for everything. During their first six months of courting, he was very attentive to her. They got married and he moved into her apartment.

Lori said that as soon as Tony moved in, he became a different person. He started to belittle and neglect her. Yet she continued to pay all the bills, bought him a new wardrobe, and gave him free access to her bank accounts. He had a lot of anger in him and would take it out on her. He came home at all hours of the morning. When she would inquire as to where he had been, he would tell her it was none of her business.

Tony decided to take yoga and new-age classes, which she paid for. He would run up their phone bill to over three hundred dollars per month calling various psychic hotlines for advice. Whenever she spoke to him about his overspending, he withheld sex from her and told her "his psychic" had said she was not up to his "spiritual level." He always told her that as soon as he "made it big" he was going to leave her. However, when she threatened that she would leave him, he cried and apologized. Then she would buy him more gifts, including two-hundred-dollar leather boots, three-hundred-dollar leather pants, and four-hundred-dollar leather jackets. But after a couple of weeks, the cycle would start again.

Lori had by now lost her self-esteem, and she continued in this unhealthy marriage. At one point Tony told her she needed to get away to "get her head together" because she had to "lift herself to a higher spiritual level" in order to deal with him. She was distraught, but, following his instructions, she went to Florida for two weeks. When she returned, she found strands of blond hair in her bed and bathroom (his hair is dark). She confronted him about his cheating. He admitted it and once again begged for forgiveness. She stayed and continued to give him a weekly allowance of five hundred dollars "to pursue his music career." She finally realized that his "music career" consisted of sitting in front of the TV all day watching soap operas, MTV, and talk shows—and at night, going out drinking and smoking marijuana with friends. In short, she was supporting his entertainment habits.

SIS, IT'S TIME TO DROP THE ZERO AND GET A HERO

One night Tony came home very drunk. They argued, and he called Lori a "black bitch." She told him she had had enough and was not going to support him anymore. She had threatened to leave many times in the past and had not followed through, so he called her bluff and told her to go ahead.

This time Lori was serious. Through some friends, she made arrangements to go to Las Vegas. After two weeks she left. Tony called her every day, crying and begging her to come home, telling her he couldn't live without her. He promised he would change and get a job to help pay the bills. After twelve weeks, she returned to New York. She realized now why he had been pressuring her to come back—the rent and utilities had not been paid for the three months she had been away.

When she came to my workshop, "How to Attract a Stable and Reliable Mate in Your Life," she had been back from Las Vegas for eight weeks and Tony had not made any attempt to find a job. After she shared her story and asked what she should do, I gave her a straightforward answer that I hoped would jolt her into reclaiming her dignity:

"Tony is not a husband. He is a gigolo. You are actually begging him to stay—paying him to love you. By doing so, you have surrendered all your self-love, dignity, and pride. You have given your power away to someone who is selfishly using you to boost up his own faltering ego.

"He has found an easy ride in life—an alternative to getting a real job—and he goes for broke. You have become his ATM—automatic teller machine. He automatically withdraws your cash by pushing your buttons. So, why should he work? You are his financier—his "sugar mama." While you are making withdrawals from your account to supply his needs, he's making deposits into his, to fulfill his wants.

"When you are broke and crying alone, he will leave you and find the next ATM sister. Why should he get a nine-to-five, when he has you "twenty-four/ seven," paying for his presence in your life? Sis, this man is a charity case. If you want to give away your money like that, then please at least give to a good cause. Find a poor, underprivileged kid and help finance his or her education. Stop playing the helpless victim here. Exercise your will and take responsibility for the choice you have made—now make the conscientious commitment to yourself, as a beautiful and valuable sister, and get rid of this user."

REFUSE TO BE USED

Being duped by a dishonest lover is bad enough. But being duped and broke is double defeat. You can refuse to be used—and choose to pick better. Invest your money in you. Stop feeling sorry for yourself. Stop thinking that you can't do any better—you can. Whenever you feel down about yourself, think of the old and wise saying, "I felt sorry for myself because I didn't have any shoes, until I met the man who didn't have any feet."

In other words, count your blessings. Make positive affirmations like these to yourself:

1. "I love and approve of myself exactly as I am."
2. "I now find effective solutions to every challenge in my life."
3. "I feel valuable, courageous, successful, and bold."

Make up your own positive statements to yourself on a daily basis. To experience any worthwhile relationship, you must first like who you are.

IF YOU WANT TO BE CHERISHED, YOU MUST FIRST LEARN TO CHERISH YOURSELF

Of all your relationships, the most important one you will ever have is the one with yourself. You spend more time with yourself than you can ever spend with another. But how many of us actually like ourselves? We have let other people define who we are. We can't look to the media or to the general public for approval. Black women are constantly being subliminally programmed that we are less than ideal—we are too dark, too light, too tall, too short, too fat, too flat-chested, or any other "too's" that do not fit the American ideal. Each one of us has got to accept and appreciate her own individual and unique beautiful self.

If you are in a situation where you are allowing yourself to be used as a man's breadwinner, stop fooling yourself that everything is hunky-dory. It won't be when the "hunk-y" walks out the "door-y" and leaves you broke, sore, and sorry. Nobody, and I mean nobody, is "fine" enough to cause you to put yourself down. Because when you put someone up on a pedestal, you're actually keeping yourself down.

IS THE TOY BOY'S SEXUAL DRAMA WORTH THE LOVE OF YOUR MAMA?

Too many of us have bought into ridiculous stereotypes and have put ourselves and our own looks down. A very disgraceful thing that many sisters do to themselves is worship and pay for a man's body, looks, or youth. Many sisters complain to me that attractive men use their looks to take advantage of and manipulate them. They claim these brothers are "gold diggers" who use sisters for their money. This is nonsense! Although those guys are con artists, you must take responsibility for your actions. You can be used in this manner only if you allow yourself to be used.

Forty-nine-year-old Majorie is walking straight into a rattrap with her eyes wide open. She shares that she has been seeing thirty-four-year-old Peter for fourteen months. She rents a spacious duplex apartment in which her seventy-two-year-old mother has been living with her for six years. Peter, who earns much less than Majorie does, suggested that they move in together so he can save money and someday "maybe" buy her an engagement ring. He said he would only move in under one condition . . .

MAJORIE: This is the first man I've met in a long time who I'm happy with. He wants to move in, but he says my mother has to move out first. *(Pause)*

DR. CORNISH: So what do you plan to do?

MAJORIE: I don't know. I've finally found someone who loves me. This may be my last chance at love; I am not getting any younger. I can't let him go. I love my mother, but I can't let her block my chance of being happy. It's not that she'll be out in the street or anything. She can go and live with my brother and his wife. Even though my mother and my sister-in-law don't get along, they have to take her now because I have had her for the past six years.

DR. CORNISH: I don't understand; why does he want your mother to leave?

MAJORIE: When he comes over we can have sex only in my bedroom. He said he wants to feel uninhibited. And he wants us to be free to have sex in the living room or on the dining table if the mood hits him.

DR. CORNISH: That's the reason? If you want to get your groove on with your young lover, go for it, but to kick your own mother out for him or anyone else is inhuman and ridiculous. If he really loves you, as he claims, you could both put your money together and rent a larger house with enough space where your mother could live peacefully and you could have your privacy. What kind of man would suggest putting out a seventy-two-year-old woman? I strongly suggest you look carefully at what you are getting into before you make a tragic mistake.

REFUSE TO BE A SISTA IN DISTRESS AND YOU CAN GET RID OF THE UNNECESSARY MESS

When sisters come to me for consultations, after we clear away the surface debris and get to the core, we find out that it isn't that they necessarily feel the guy is so great, but that they feel that they themselves are not good enough. The real issue is using a guy as a Band-Aid to cover up some deep wounds.

Someone may have hurt you somewhere along the way, and you've not liked yourself very much since. You have belittled yourself—cramped your abilities. You've got to turn yourself loose, sis! Get out from under this cloud. Stop covering your wounds. Openly face them so you can heal. It's time to clean house. To regain your self-respect, you have to get rid of anyone who is using you. Don't be afraid of being alone for a little while. You need to take a few months to define what you really want in life. Take a short break to get yourself together.

YOU'VE GOT TO CHECK YOURSELF BEFORE YOU WRECK YOURSELF

Twenty-three-year-old Joycelyn learned this the hard way. She had a bad breakup with her boyfriend of seventeen months. He left her during the Fourth of July weekend; by July 19, she was involved with a new boyfriend.

Joycelyn started seeing twenty-nine-year-old Rodney on the rebound. They met at a bus stop in her neighborhood. She worked as a cosmetic salesperson and makeup artist in a department store. She made enough money to have her own apartment and take care of herself. Rodney, on the other hand, had no job.

She used him as an escape, to avoid facing the hurt she was feeling from her previous breakup. Rodney spent every night at her apartment and moved in a a few pieces of clothing at a time. But by August 15, he had moved all of his belongings into her apartment. By the time she recognized the reality of his occupancy, four months had passed. It was too late; he had already taken up residency.

Rodney still had no job and showed no effort to seek employment. He did nothing around the house but eat, watch TV, and have sex with Jocelyn. She paid all the bills. After nine months, she got fed up with supporting him and asked him to leave. He refused and became verbally abusive. She called the police to have him taken out of her apartment; they told her they could not do anything about it because he had been living there for over thirty days. And by law, that automatically qualified him as a resident, not a visitor. She was stuck with the freeloader.

Joycelyn endured the agony of Rodney's constant abuse. But one day he almost choked her to death, and a neighbor heard the commotion and called the police. They came and arrested him. Jocelyn finally was able to get the legal papers to keep Rodney away from her. Within two weeks he moved in with another sister, a single mother with two small children, who lived up the block from her.

What a mess. Jocelyn was "thrown from the frying pan" by one lover, yet she "jumped into the fire" by her own free will. She should have given herself time to understand what had happened and to heal before prematurely going into another relationship.

Too many of us proceed to hop carelessly from one bad experience to another, to another, creating a domino effect of ill-fated romances. Instead of using a man as a Kleenex to tissue our tears away, we must stop wiping away the pain and go to the source of it to find out why we are hurting in the first place. If we would take even a short three-month celibacy break between painful experiences, to properly make peace with ourselves and get the hurt out of our systems, we would save ourselves a lot of harm.

MAKE A PLEDGE TO RENEW AND BECOME A BETTER YOU

There are two types of celibacy—voluntary celibacy and involuntary celibacy.

Voluntary celibacy occurs when you choose to take a break from relationships (for at least three months) to find out more about yourself. About your own personal wants and needs. It's a loving, nurturing, and sometimes spiritual trip—something like seeking the kingdom within. What's really rewarding about this is that you find out important things about yourself that you may never have known. About how much you enjoy your own space, your own peace of mind. You explore new hobbies and new interests. You realize how creative you are. You take time to nurture and pamper yourself. This gives you a healthy sense of self and prepares you for a healthy bonding with a deserving partner. You may even decide to enjoy your own space and growth for years. This is a fascinating journey of self-discovery.

Involuntary celibacy occurs when you are forced into being by yourself because of an estranged lover or when you have retreated to escape from the hurt of a relationship gone sour. With this type of celibacy you are lonely, sad, angry, and/or bitter. In this state, you are left with feelings of fear and rejection. You are unable to trust. And in order to protect yourself, you build a barrier to keep others from getting in. But in doing so you also keep yourself from getting out. This one is a defeating trip of self-pity.

The former celibacy is healthy and empowers us; the latter is unhealthy and discourages us. If you are presently in the involuntary celibacy state, you can turn it into a positive experience by learning how to embrace, enjoy, and enhance who you truly are. If not, you may eventually get entangled in another unbalanced relationship if you fail to analyze what went wrong and why.

WHY DID YOU GO FOR A GIGOLO BRO?

To find out what compels sisters to pay to keep a man, I surveyed two hundred sisters. Some have been jilted by men they have kept in the past, and others are presently in relationships with men they are financially supporting. I got a wide range and interesting mix of responses, but I categorized them in the following four ways. Each of these men can prompt a sister to use her finance to maintain his romance:

1. *The Cover Boy* He is incredibly handsome. He is also referred to as a "pretty boy." She is swept away by his exceptionally good looks. She enjoys the admiration other women bestow on him, and feels he is a prize to be won. In this case, she maintains him because he looks good on her arm. She needs him as her trophy.

2. *The Lover Boy* This brother is usually a "roaming Romeo." He is a lady's man in the truest sense. He is very charming and smooth. It is no secret that he has many women, but she wants to be the one woman who reforms him. This gives her a sense of being number one and having an edge over the others. In this case, she maintains him because she feels special to be able to pry him away from other women. She needs him as her ego booster.

3. *The Joy Boy* If you looked in the dictionary under "sex appeal," you would find this brother described to the letter. He possesses a sensuous and natural animal magnetism. He is clean yet rugged, rude yet alluring. He is an intoxicating blend of fire and ice—with a mesmerizing sexual attraction that bids you "come hither." In this case, she maintains him because he satisfies her sexually. She needs him as her sex object.

4. *The Toy Boy* He is much younger than she is. She feels privileged because with all the younger attractive women out there,

he has chosen to be with her. In most cases, the woman has had to work hard all of her life and never had a chance to enjoy her own youth; he makes her feel as if she is making up for what she missed earlier. He makes her feel young again. She is now what's described as the "recycled teenager." In this case, she maintains him because he helps her to recapture her youth. She needs him as her fountain of youth.

Whatever the type of man she selected, in every case the sister needed to cover her own inadequacy. The brother was just the paid hand who filled her emptiness. Any time you have to pay a man to love you, no matter how subtle the payment, something is wrong. Take stock of yourself and place a high value on yourself. Realize that you deserve to have a compassionate lover who thinks well enough of you to look out for your best interest— instead of one who tries to squeeze you dry like an orange in a juice extractor.

FALLING PREY TO THE "BAIT AND SWITCH" SHAM

Have you ever seen something you really wanted being advertised at an incredible price, but found that the item was already gone by the time you got to the store? It's very disappointing and annoying, isn't it?

A common practice that retail stores and supermarkets use to lure buyers in is the old "bait and switch" trick. A quality product is advertised at a remarkable sales price, which makes it seem like a must-have purchase. In actuality, there are only a few of the advertised items there to begin with. So when you get to the store, you don't find the item that brought you there in the first place. They tell you that they are all sold out, but that they have substituted a "comparable" item. The comparable item is usually of lower quality and sometimes higher-priced. You may initially be disappointed, but since you are already in the store, you decide you might as well stay and shop—you end up taking the bait.

So it is with the bait-and-switch lover. He has a well-thought-out plan to manipulate himself into the lives of as many women as possible. It's as if he's trying to gain entry into the Guinness Book of Records. He wines and dines you for the first few dates. Then, when he believes you are hooked, he switches. He moves on to the next sister, yet keeps you hanging on.

BEING EASILY IMPRESSED MAY ONE DAY LEAVE YOU PENNILESS

Thirty-eight-year-old Pearl has a successful career as a real-estate broker. She met forty-five-year-old William when he put one of his two homes on the market. It was sold through her company within a short time. He invited her out to dinner to celebrate the sale, then called her every day for the next two weeks—they saw each other four times each week in this period. During this time, Pearl found out that William was a very wealthy black man who owned a lucrative landscaping and contracting business. Their first Sunday together, he invited her to his home in the suburbs for a cocktail brunch. It was a nine-bedroom baby mansion with a three-car garage housing a Rolls-Royce, a Jaguar, and a Range Rover.

Pearl was impressed by William's possessions and decided this was the man of her dreams. During the first fourteen days, she had his undivided attention. He asked her if she would like to be the special woman in his life. She replied, "Definitely." He shared with her that because of his wealth, women were always trying to get him to marry them, and he was looking for a good woman who didn't want to use him for his financial worth. That was the woman who would be his wife. But after that declaration (the bait), he cut back on seeing her, and called her only about once a week (the switch).

The less William called her, the more determined Pearl became to show him that she was different from "all the other women." She set out to prove that she didn't need, and wasn't after, his riches. So, she began to buy him gifts—lots of gifts—expensive gifts.

He stopped inviting her out to dinner, but instead invited her to his home for dinner, and always asked her to pick up something on the way over to cook. She would use her money to buy his groceries, and she would cook the meals for him. But she didn't mind. She believed she was proving to him what good "wife material" she was. So continued their relationship for several months.

During one of their meals, William discreetly hinted that his birthday was approaching, and that he wanted her to organize and finance a big "surprise" birthday bash for him. She was only too happy to comply, believing that this would seal her position as "the one" in front of all his friends and family. He gave her a list of names that amounted to 140 guests.

WHOEVER SAID "MONEY BEGETS MONEY" COULD NOT HAVE BEEN REFERRING TO THIS . . .

Pearl decided she would make this a birthday William could never forget. She would buy only the very best and spare no expense. His house, although tastefully decorated, was somewhat empty inside. She decided to add a few statement pieces. The few statement pieces included an eighteenth-century mahogany dining-room set, a double-pedestal table, Chippendale chairs, and a carved four-poster bed. She spent just under $19,000 for the decorating alone—plus an additional $4,200 to have the party catered.

Although the "surprise" party was to be in William's honor, Pearl also received a surprise. William had conveniently forgotten to mention that he had been married twice before and had five grown children in their twenties, as well as a sixth child—a seven-year-old daughter—and a few special "lady friends." All of these people were among the invited guests.

Pearl was very hurt by this discovery. But she was still determined to be the future "Mrs. William." Her displeasure intensified when she overheard two of William's daughters whispering about "how much Daddy has managed to get out of this new one." At this point she left the party. But the following week, after William had dropped the same line about looking for a wife who was not out to use him, she was back making him Sunday brunch.

It's been almost two years since the start of their relationship. Pearl knows that William sees other women. She is not pleased about it, but she continues to buy him gifts to prove that she is the right one for him.

From on the outside, looking in, we can easily ask why Pearl doesn't just let go, since she knows the type of person she is involved with.

If You Go for the Bait, You Will Get Caught

Let me share an experience with you. I remember going on weekend fishing trips in the country with an old boyfriend some years ago. When he ran out of live bait, he used plastic bait instead, and he caught just as many fish as with the real thing.

Out of curiosity, I asked him, "With all the things in the sea to eat, why does the fish come to your plastic bait even though it's not real food?"

"They don't know the difference," he explained. "All you need to use is something shiny to get their attention."

"But when the fish bites and you pull up and it's not yet hooked," I probed, "why does it keep coming back and nibbling on plastic?"

"That's a good question," he commented. "I never thought about it before. I guess it's because of greed."

Greed. Pearl is motivated by greed. She has seen what William has, and she is determined to have it for herself. She was blinded by shiny prospects of his surface worth—plastic. She never bothered to look into the real wealth—his character. Little does she realize that con artist William is one step ahead of her in this defeating game. He uses his surface wealth to entrap women to support him. Is it any wonder he is so rich? It's the oldest trick in the book: Set the bait, get them to nibble, hook them, and reel them in. It's just a pity that a man would do such an undignified thing. And an even bigger pity that a sister would spend her money so foolishly. The man doesn't have to pay for anything anymore. He has caught quite a few "fish" to maintain his lifestyle.

You know there must be a fine line between being greedy and being foolish. Because if Pearl would wise up, she would realize that the tens of thousands of dollars she's invested into William's growing wealth could eventually have been part of a down payment on her own baby mansion.

If you ever feel you are "hooked" by one who threatens to leave you, declaring, "There are a lot of fish in the sea," tell him to "Go fish," because "There are a lot of fishermen in the ocean, too." So you don't ever have to worry about being stuck with a dysfunctional "fisherman."

WHY NOT DROP THE DEADWEIGHT AND GO FOR THE HEAVYWEIGHT?

Sharing with a good man who shares with you is a healthy union. But being with a sponge who absorbs all he can get from you is deplorable. Get rid of the user. Users are losers. You were not put on this earth to become a doormat for anyone to walk all over. You are too important an individual to foolishly throw away your hard-earned money like that. Money is power. Don't just carelessly give yours away. What you need to give away is the deadweight lover.

Why settle for less, when it takes the same effort to go for the best? From now on go for a heavyweight mate.

The Ten Disadvantages of Dating a Deadweight

He:

1. Is constantly "between" jobs and never working.
2. Asks you for loans, but never pays them back.
3. Never pays for dates, even when he invites you out.
4. Dictates how you should spend your own money.
5. Asks you to buy him gifts, yet never buys you any.
6. Expects you to pay his bills.
7. Takes your kindness as weakness.
8. Always finds ways to *take away* your best.
9. Tells you how lucky you are to have him.
10. Is a "walking liability" who always holds *your* own.

The Ten Advantages of Having a Heavyweight

He:

1. Has his own satisfactory job.
2. Has his own bank accounts and balances his own checkbooks.
3. Always pays for dates when he asks you out.
4. Does not interfere with how you spend your own money.
5. Buys you gifts, yet never pressures you into buying him any.
6. Pays his own bills.
7. Takes your kindness as sweetness.
8. Always finds ways to *bring out* your best.
9. Tells you how lucky he feels to have you.
10. Is a "walking asset" who always holds *his* own.

Self-Worth Is Yours for the Asking

Reclaim your power and respect. Don't ever feel that you are alone. You are not alone. I, for one, am in your corner. Commit this affirmation to memory. Let's call it the decree of the modern-day sisterhood:

> *I will not let anyone leave me*
> *abused, confused, and feeling misused.*
> *I will not let any man leave me*
> *broke, alone, and singing the blues.*

Come on, sis—pick yourself up, sit yourself down; do whatever it takes to reclaim your self-worth. I know you can do it. Be kind to yourself. Never love a man who does not cherish you—LOSE THE USER AND CHOOSE A CHAMPION!

bad choice

6

Staying On, Although Respect Has Gone

An equal balance of respect and love is the formula for an ideal relationship. But if I had to make a choice of which is more important in a relationship, I would choose respect over love any day. If someone respects you, he'll appreciate your worth and treat you kindly. However, too often people have declared "love" for each other, yet possession, jealousy, and obsession entered into their relationships.

Many sisters have endured mental, emotional, and physical abuse, and when asked why, they answer, "because I loved him." What's equally amazing is when abusers declare "love" as the justification for their crimes. They frequently say that they beat up their wives and girlfriends out of love.

If the respect had substituted for love in these cases, there would have been no abuse. Because when someone respects you, they honor your right as an individual to make your own decisions and have your own preferences. They do not attempt to deprive you of your right to live your life as you choose; they do not force their opinions on you. Nor do they make you submit to their demands by using physical force. Most importantly, they do not hurt or even try to kill you if you decide you no longer want to have a relationship with them.

People are more likely to abuse someone they feel superior to—someone they feel they own. You can't "own" someone whom you respect as an individual, because respect implies feeling that someone is your equal. Too many sisters have been victimized and brutalized because their assailants' definitions of "love" read "ownership and control."

"WHAT'S LOVE GOT TO DO WITH IT?"

When popular recording artist Tina Turner released the song "What's Love Got to Do with It?", it immediately catapulted to the top of music charts around the globe. This sister had endured her own hellish nightmare with an abusive husband for years. Had she not fled for her life, she probably would not have been alive to sing this song of survival which struck such a familiar chord deep within millions of us.

The movie about Tina Turner's life, with the same title as the song, shows the tragic abuse that so many sisters are enduring at this very moment. National statistics reflect that more black women are killed by abusive current or ex-boyfriends, lovers, and husbands than by strangers or accidents.

I've lost both my mother and my aunt because they were murdered by control addicts. My mother was killed by an obsessive ex-boyfriend turned stalker who refused to let go, my aunt by a possessive live-in lover who refused to get out.

What would cause an abuser to commit so heinous a crime is research for another book. My concern here is to help sisters who are presently being victimized to get out, and to prevent others from getting into any form of abusive relationship—be it emotional, verbal, or physical.

TRAGEDY TRIGGERS A CHAIN REACTION OF PAIN THROUGH THE PEOPLE CLOSEST TO YOU

My mother's death subconsciously haunted me for years. I say subconsciously because although I witnessed her death at age ten, I blocked it out completely until I was twenty-four—the age at which I experienced a major turning point in my life. However, as I'm sharing this with you now, with deep sincerity and openness, it's very vivid in my memory. I'm going to walk you through her brief story and tragic end.

My mother was Rosalie, a popular fashion model of the late sixties and early seventies. Her full name was Rosalie Yvonne Owen. Although she had been married and divorced, she had never changed her name. She was very pretty, charming, and financially successful. She was one of the first black women ever to model for Bloomingdale's, and she was in great demand among the fashion houses in Europe, where she was affectionately dubbed the "Black Diamond."

The man who murdered my mother was someone she had known for years but had dated for only a short period of time. When she started dating him, his obsession for her became overbearing, so she broke it off and told him they could only be friends and nothing more. He refused to take no for an answer. On several occasions he told her, "I'm already in love with you, so it's too late." She refused to let him bully her into being with him and repeatedly asked him to stay away from her. He told her he never would.

IF SOMEONE THREATENS YOU, BELIEVE HIM! TAKE LEGAL ACTION BEFORE IT'S TOO LATE!

On the morning of July 11, 1972, my mother was doing in-store modeling for Bloomingdale's. My eleven-year-old sister, Angie, and I (I was ten at the time) were at home with our live-in nanny, Fiona, whom my mother had brought over from England to take care of us. My cousin Michelle, eight, was spending the day with us. At about 11:30 in the morning, Michelle and I were watching TV in the living room and Angie was in her bedroom, when the doorbell rang. Fiona opened the door, and the man walked in before she could stop him. Angie knew my mother didn't want him around, but I had no clue about their disagreement. Angie said to him, "My mother isn't here. I don't think you should be here." He responded, "Your mother is expecting me. She will be home soon."

YOU MUST PUT OUT A WARNING TO EVERYONE NOT TO LET AN OFFENDER INTO YOUR HOME

Angie had a suspicious look on her face as she went back into her bedroom. The man had a brown paper bag in his hand and came into the living room, sat down on the couch, and watched TV with Michelle and me. He put the paper bag on the floor right next to his feet. About half an hour had passed when he asked me, "Did your mother say what time she would be home?" "No. What's in the bag?" I asked while reaching for the paper bag. "No, no, no, don't touch that!" he said quickly, grabbing the bag from the floor. "It's something for grown-ups."

I returned my attention to the TV. Another hour passed before the phone rang. I ran to answer it. It was my mother calling to check how we were doing. "Hi, Mommy, guess who's here?" I couldn't wait to tell her. "He said you are expecting him." (She wasn't.)

"Where is he?" she asked, almost in a whisper.

"He's sitting right here on the sofa."

"Where are Angie and Fiona?"

"They are in their bedrooms."

"Let me speak to both of them first, then I'll speak to him."

"Are you coming home soon?"

"Yes, sweetheart. Let me speak to your sister, but tell her to pick up the phone in my bedroom."

"Okay. Hold on," I said. At this point, the man anxiously extended his hand for the phone. "She wants to speak to Angie first," I said. I went and told Angie, and I returned to watch TV with Michelle. After my mother had spoken to Angie and Fiona, Angie came to tell the visitor to pick up the phone. He left the living room and went to use the extension in the kitchen, which was out of our hearing range.

About five minutes later he returned, singing the lyrics, "Alone again naturally."

A CONTROL ADDICT WILL THREATEN TO KILL YOUR LOVED ONES TO GET YOU TO SUBMIT TO HIM

Within forty-five minutes my mother was home. She had come home early. The minute her ex-boyfriend heard her come through the door, he sprang to his feet, still clutching the paper bag. She walked past him and came over to kiss Michelle and me, then went toward Angie's bedroom. He followed behind her. Michelle and I continued to be engrossed in the TV.

I heard faint voices that sounded like they were arguing, but I wasn't quite sure, so I continued watching the TV. Gradually, as the voices got louder, Michelle and I took our attention away from the TV and listened to the confrontation that was going on down the corridor from us.

He kept on repeating, "I love you. You have to marry me. I need you in my life. I told you before, I will never let you go."

AN ABUSER DOESN'T UNDERSTAND "NO"; HE ONLY HEARS WHAT HE WANTS TO HEAR

My mother kept saying, "Why are you doing this? I have told you I am not in love with you. Just please leave me alone. Just leave me and my kids and go on with your life."

What followed next took place so fast, yet now it seems like it was an eternity. "Please don't hurt my mother," I heard Angie cry. "It's okay, Angie. Get out the way, love—get behind me," my mother urged.

"If I can't have you, no one else will," he shouted. Then I heard—Boom, Boom, Boom—gunshots and screaming coming from everywhere! "Jesus Christ, he shot her! He shot her! He shot her!" Fiona was screaming. Angie screamed, "Don't kill me!" Michelle and I were clutching each other, crying and trembling with fear as Angie ran for her life with him chasing behind her. As he was running past the living room, he turned toward us with the gun in his hand and a wild look on his face—then he pointed the gun directly at us. Michelle and I hugged each other tightly, frightened and begging for our lives, crying, "Don't kill us! Please don't kill us! We didn't do anything to you! Please don't kill us!" He just froze for a moment—just stood there with the loaded gun pointed at us and that horrible look on his face—while we screamed in horror.

His attention was distracted from us by Angie's terrified plea from the outside doorway: "Please don't kill my sister. Please leave them alone! Don't kill them!" He turned and ran after her.

In fear, Michelle ran behind the couch. Fiona was screaming hysterically through my bedroom window—"He killed her! Oh, God, please, help! Somebody call the police! He killed her!"

Hysterical, I ran down the corridor to look for my mother. She was lying on her stomach, feet toward me, with her head turned left, facing the the wall nearest the guest room. (The paper bag he had brought the gun in was on the floor next to her body.)

I ran over to her and knelt by her right side—I was facing the back of her head. I was in a daze and thought that she had been shot in her back and had fallen on her stomach. But I was confused because I didn't see any blood coming from her back. I ran my hand over her back, feeling for wounds. I didn't find any. I was hoping that she was just pretending to be hurt—just lying still—just to make him think she was dead, so he would leave and not come back.

I whispered in her ear, still crying with fear, "Mommy, he's gone; you can get up now." But she didn't move. She made a faint moan, and I shook her shoulder and repeated, "Mommy, it's okay now, he's not here anymore." She didn't respond. Since I didn't see any blood, I couldn't understand why she just wouldn't get up. "Mommy, why don't you answer me?" I pleaded. She moaned again, and her head twitched slightly. I wanted to see her face to find out why she wasn't answering me. I leaned over to see her face, and I saw the stream of blood flowing from her left temple. "Oh, God, no. God, please don't let my mother die. Mommy, please get up. Mommy, don't leave me. . . . Please don't die. . . ."

Her death certificate stated the immediate cause of death: "Bullet wounds of head, neck, and brain." The media report: "Fashion model Rosalie shot to death by obsessive ex-boyfriend who killed himself immediately after in the lobby of her building."

NEVER LEAVE YOUR LIFE IN THE HANDS OF FATE; TAKE MATTERS INTO YOUR OWN HANDS AND GET THE PROPER HELP

Reliving this story has taken me on an incredible journey. My purpose in reaching into my personal experience and sharing my own mother's story with you is to give you the courage to get out of any abusive relationship immediately!

Please don't jeopardize one more day of your life—don't make the mistake my mother made by hoping the abuser will eventually leave you alone. If someone threatens your life and refuses to leave you alone, get the proper legal authorities to deal with him.

What's especially frightening is that most of the time these are not strangers. They are often friends whom you have known for years. An obsessive stalker is cunning, calculating, and mentally unbalanced—you cannot handle him on your own. This man had made up his mind that if my mother wouldn't agree that they should live together, he would make sure they died together.

How anyone could be so obsessed with another human being that their own life means nothing to them without the other person is still puzzling to me. But it is a reality. At this very moment there are thousands of sisters being brutalized or hunted by control freaks.

THE TWO TYPES OF CONTROL ADDICTS

There are two distinct characteristics of control addicts. One type is obsessive, and the other is possessive.

The *obsessive* person lives his life through his chosen victim. He has convinced himself that his life is useless without her. He is completely consumed with her and needs her to fill his emptiness and save his faltering ego. If his victim doesn't give in to his demands he may eventually kill her, and he generally doesn't care whether he lives or dies afterward. My mother's killer had this personality type.

The *possessive* person demands that his chosen victim live her life through him. He attempts to convince her that her life is useless without him. He demands that she be completely consumed with him, and he uses her to cover his insecurities and boost his overinflated ego. In this case, if she refuses to obey his orders, he may eventually take her life, but he usually tries to escape and get away with the murder. My aunt's killer had this personality type.

Both of these personality types are equally self-centered and narcissistic; both are equally deadly and dangerous.

TEN WARNING SIGNS THAT IDENTIFY A BORDERLINE CONTROL FREAK

1. He constantly pays you unexpected visits, even after you've asked him not to.

2. He wants to know your every move—he calls at least three times a day for an update of your activities.

3. He tries to keep you away from your friends and family.

4. He has frequent temper tantrums and is unable to control his anger.

5. He is extremely jealous of you.

6. He believes women are subservient to men—he believes you are his property.

7. He wants to make all your decisions for you.

8. He is very vengeful and enjoys other people's setbacks.

9. He gets offended when you don't agree with his opinions.

10. He has a history of domestic violence from his past relationships.

WHOEVER SAID "DON'T AIR YOUR DIRTY LAUNDRY OUT IN PUBLIC" SUFFERED FROM A MASSIVE DOSE OF FALSE PRIDE

What I find extremely alarming is the number of sisters who would rather stay in life-threatening relationships than seek help from a friend, or anyone, because they are too embarrassed to "air their dirty laundry out in public." Most would rather suffer in silence, pretending all is well, being battered behind closed doors, than have people "in their business."

Look, sis, if you are being hurt, lose the false pride and save your life! Too many sisters are being slaughtered and butchered because of false pride.

This apparently is what happened to my aunt. Aunt Gloria was a beautiful, divorced, professional, and financially secure sister. She was forty-seven when she was introduced to the man who would one year later become her live-in lover and three years later become her murderer. She was a nurse who owned her own home, and she was just looking for companionship. She met this man through his cousin, who had been a longtime casual friend of hers. They started dating. Gradually, under his direction, she became distant from her family and friends. He kept telling her they were jealous of her happiness. She bought into his sham and completely isolated herself from everyone, including her two grown children. Shortly after, he moved into her house.

Don't Worry What Others Are Thinking About; Just Get Yourself Out—Before He Takes You Out

Living with this man, Aunt Gloria realized what his true personality was like, as he started abusing her. But she was too embarrassed to tell anyone. No one knew what she was going through, because she kept silent.

On the morning of her fiftieth birthday, he stabbed her to death, forty times in all, with a butcher knife. As he stabbed her, he "somehow" cut himself on his left hand. After he murdered her, he called 911 and reported, "I just killed my wife; come and get me. I don't remember what happened. I didn't know what I was doing."

The Act of a Calculating and Controlling Con Artist

Because the man had a cut on his hand, he was put in a transitional hospital to heal before he was sent to jail. He had access to a phone in his hospital room. On the day of Aunt Gloria's funeral, he called her house. When her daughter (my cousin) answered the phone, he took her by surprise and told her that he was calling to make sure his belongings were safe. He said that he was going to get one of his friends to come to the house for them, to put them in storage for a few years. (Can you believe this?)

My cousin was numbed and grief-stricken, and she asked him why he had killed her mother. He just sighed and said, "It's a long story; you wouldn't understand." She became hysterical and hung up on him.

I was in Europe on a lecture tour when I got this tragic news. I flew back immediately to pay my respects and to try to fit the pieces of the puzzle together. I was unable to get any more detail than what I've shared with you, all because Aunt Gloria was too embarrassed to seek help. She covered it up and pretended all was well, and no one knew. Her killer pleaded "temporary insanity" at the trial and may one day get out on parole.

WARNING: WHEN YOU ARE GONE, HE'LL JUST MOVE ON TO THE NEXT VICTIM—SO BREAK THE PATTERN NOW

Isn't that something? Aunt Gloria had her life snuffed out by this control freak, and he may be set free to perform another slaughter on some other unsuspecting sister someday.

Sis, make sure it isn't you. Do not ever keep silent about abuse. I've never been hit by a lover before in my life—and I have no intention of it ever happening to me. But, if it should ever happen, I would be the first one out the door and the first one to report his abuse. Then, I would send him to a fellow psychologist to seek help. I would never cover for an abusive lover, and neither should you. You are too valuable a human being to be disrespected like this.

IT'S BETTER TO BE ALIVE WITH A LITTLE "DIRTY LAUNDRY" THAN TO BE DEAD WITH ALL THE "CLEAN LINEN" IN THE WORLD

There is nothing to be ashamed about. Don't hide someone's abuse toward you. Don't ever feel guilty or embarrassed for his behavior. You are not responsible for his actions, but you are responsible for yours. And if you sit there motionless, allowing him to continue his abuse just because you are worried about what other people may think, then you may be preparing yourself for an early grave.

Let me tell you something I learned many years ago: The very same people you may be trying to impress by pretending all is well are usually experiencing their own private nightmares behind closed doors. But they also pretend all is well because of fear of what other people will think.

If you strongly believe that you can't confide in these people because they are the sort of warped individuals who will laugh at someone's suffering, then bid them good riddance. Because you don't need friends who are cruel and hardened anyway. If you need immediate help, call one of the referral numbers I have listed at the end of the book. You must get out and get help. I promise you, it will get better. There is so much truth to this wise quote: "Weeping may endure for a night, but joy cometh in the morning."

WE ARE OUR SISTERS' KEEPERS

If you sense that a friend is going through some form of abuse but is embarrassed to talk about it, please be kind—lend her a helping hand. Don't avoid the issue. Gradually get her to open up to you— or show her this section of the book. Let her know that she is not alone and that there is no shame in trying to get out of a dangerous liaison. The only shame is not getting her out soon enough to save her life.

YOU CAN'T CURE HIS FATAL ATTRACTION; HE CONTROLS YOU FOR HIS OWN SELFISH SATISFACTION

I cannot begin to tell you how frustrating it is when sisters remain in terminal relationships, jeopardizing their lives, believing their abusive lovers will eventually change.

The abusers always refuse to get help, and the sisters become codependent fixtures. The abusers are usually mastermind manipulators and have managed to brainwash their victims into feeling responsible for the abuse.

Thirty-year-old Lynne has been enduring abuse from Patrick, her thirty-two-year-old live-in boyfriend, for two years. During this time, she has been in the hospital several times after Patrick's beatings. She has had broken ribs, a broken eardrum, and fractured shoulders. Each time she threatens to leave, he apologizes and buys her jewelry, flowers, or perfume to bribe her into forgiving him. She keeps giving in to his pleas, telling herself, "He really means it this time."

REFUSE TO EXCUSE HIS CONSTANT ABUSE

Although Lynne claimed Patrick was trying to change and hadn't physically battered her for four months, she was still worried because he had developed a new form of "punishment."

LYNNE: He has been grounding me and giving me "time-out." He has locked me in the bathroom for three hours, twice. He says it's for my own protection, until his temper cools down. I can't fight him back because I can't manage him.

DR. CORNISH: Lynne, what in the world are you doing with such a calculating and controlling person? The only time-out you need is permanent time out of this volatile relationship. You were not put on this earth to be a punching bag for anyone. Let him go and take up professional boxing as a career if he wants to punch someone around—and tell him to go get a job at the zoo or in a circus as a lion tamer if he wants to practice his disciplinary skills. Time-out? This guy is way off. You need to get out of this now.

LYNNE: I know. But I still love him.

DR. CORNISH: Love? Love has nothing to do with this. This is about survival. Love him from a distance if you have to, but get out. There is no excuse for you being beaten and grounded. Would you allow your parents to ground you at this age?

LYNNE: No.

DR. CORNISH: Then why allow this guy to do this to you?

BEWARE THE DR. JEKYLL AND MR. HYDE OFFENDER

LYNNE: He becomes two different persons—as if he has a split personality. And when he's not angry he treats me nice. He wasn't like this in the beginning. I want him back the way he was before.

DR. CORNISH: I'm sure he does have a nice side to him. Or else you probably would not have been with him in the first place. But you have to face reality and stop making excuses for his abusive behavior. Stop confusing yourself by reminiscing on how he was in the past. Look at how he is behaving now. At present, he's unstable. Eventually, he may be able to change, but you can't do it for him. He needs professional therapy. But he has to be the one who wants to make the first step. And as long as he uses you as an outlet to vent his rage, he won't change.

LYNNE: I'm afraid of leaving him . . . and part of me still loves him.

DR. CORNISH: You are living in fear and he's feeding off your fear. You have allowed him to take your power away. If you insist on staying, you have to let him know you are serious about him getting professional help. If he refuses, you have to be brave and leave, or else the only thing that may be left of you is your voice on a 911 tape calling for help.

AVOID THE BROTHER-DICTATOR/SISTER-CARETAKER UNIONS

Patrick has assumed the role of the controlling dictator while Lynne plays the role of the submissive caretaker in their relationship. He is being unreasonable and unrealistic and is living in a fool's paradise. And being fearful for her life, Lynne is afraid of erasing the mirage.

His attempt to beat her into submission is deplorable. The "do as I say and not as I do" attitude is a major personality flaw of Patrick's. Any brother who wants to enslave a sister by giving her "time-out" and "grounding" her sincerely needs a strong dose of black pride and awareness to realize that our ancestors did not fight side by side to free us from the grips of social slavery for us to drop into the clutches of household slavery. A sister who chooses to stay in such a life-threatening relationship is robbing herself of the personal power we have struggled so hard to accomplish—and is also being stripped of her God-given birthright of free will.

WE'VE COME A LONG ENOUGH WAY TO HAVE OUR OWN SAY, BABY

What's especially sad about this is that all along black women have had to work side by side with black men in this country, from the earliest days of slavery, through the sharecropping period, to today's generation. A sister cannot be expected to put in fair pay and not have fair say in a relationship.

For this relationship to work, Lynne has to get Patrick to treat her fairly as a human being, and not merely as a subhuman counterpart. I agree that there are some basic differences between men and women in relationships, but even though they may not be treated equally at times, they should be treated *fairly* at all times. For instance, if Patrick wants to be the "head" of the household, that's fine, but he must respect Lynne as the "neck" of the household. Even though their input may not be equal, they are equally important, because I've never seen a head being able to stand on its own without being supported by a neck. Have you?

Both partners contribute their fair share, and both must be respected and appreciated in order to have peace and harmony in their household.

TEN POINTS TO CHECK OUT BEFORE YOU LET HIM IN

The wise saying "An ounce of prevention is better than a pound of cure" is a guideline we should all think about before rushing into relationships. We must first find out more about the man's behavioral pattern before embracing him wholeheartedly. Most black men are decent, but there are quite a few brothers with hidden agendas whom you would be much better off avoiding.

For your own protection, make sure you know the following about anyone before you get very intimate with him:

1. What is his full birth name?
2. What is his date and place of birth?
3. Where (and with whom) does he live?
4. Where does he work?
5. Where did he go to school?
6. Where do his parents or family live?
7. Has he ever been married before? If yes, is he legally divorced? For how long, and why?
8. Has he ever been arrested or had any legal troubles? If yes, what for, and why?
9. What are his beliefs about violence and infidelity?
10. What are his humanitarian or spiritual beliefs?

KNOW WHEN TO PROCEED WITH CAUTION

You can be direct and feminine at the same time. You don't have to inquire in an aggressive or a detective-style manner. No one wants to feel they are being interrogated. Just casually ease the questions into your conversation in a pleasant manner.

If he takes offense at being asked these questions, just let him know that you take pride in yourself and that you are selective about the people you let into your personal life. Tell him it's just part of getting to know each other better.

Let him know you'd be happy to answer those questions for him also. If he's still upset or apprehensive, this might be a red flag signaling that the brother has something to hide—either make a U-turn or proceed with caution!

What's the Use in Getting the Truth If You're Not Going to Put It to Good Use?

Twenty-eight-year-old Joan met her stalker through E-mail. After two weeks of computer flirting, they decided to meet in person. She did a background check on him before they met. She found out he'd been in trouble several times with the law for domestic violence and child-support court cases.

She knew he had a history, but she kept their date anyway. She continued seeing him after the first date. By the third date, they started sleeping together. After the initial six weeks of courting, he started shoving her around. Even though his abusive behavior escalated each time they saw each other, she kept saying, "One more chance."

The "one more chance" lasted five more months. After she couldn't bear his attacks anymore, she told him to leave her alone. He wouldn't take no for an answer and began stalking her. In the end, she had to get a restraining order to finally get rid of him.

Forewarned is fair-warned, sis. If you realize you'll get stung by killer bees, why purposely step into their hive?

This Makes Bungee Jumping Look Like Child's Play . . .

Twenty-four-year-old Sharon proudly admits she's attracted to the "bad boys." She boasts that she enjoys what she calls the "roughneck brothers." Her description of a thrilling time is when her current beau, after a brutal argument, held her half naked, upside down, by her ankles, over the edge of her fourteenth-floor balcony, until she agreed to have sex with him.

If Sharon wants an open-air thrill, she should take up bungee jumping instead. At least she would be secured by a safety cord, instead of having her life suspended in the palm of an enraged boyfriend's hand. For this sister's sake, I hope she gets a grip on her life before her trapeze-artist beau loses his grip on her ankles one of these days.

ONE SISTER'S DREAM BOAT IS ANOTHER SISTER'S SINKING SHIP

While sisters like Sharon are playing with their lives, sisters like Carol are running for their lives. Carol shared this about her escape from her abusive husband of six years:

"He told me whenever he hit me that it was all my fault. I used to do my best not to do or say anything that would upset him. One day he came home angry from work while I was cooking his dinner. He tried everything to get me to argue."

BEING DAMNED WHETHER YOU DO OR WHETHER YOU DON'T

"I had gotten enough beatings from him in the past to know not to say anything while he was in his mood. So I just listened and nodded in agreement with everything he said. Then all of a sudden, he just pushed me against the stove and screamed, 'What's the matter with you, bitch, are you dumb, you can't talk?' I started crying in fear and begged him not to hit me. He began laughing at me and taunted, 'Oh, so now you got your voice back, bitch!'

"He started choking me. Then he was punching and kicking me in the stomach. When I fell on the floor, I curled up in the fetal position to try to protect myself. He jumped on top of me and just started biting me all over my body. He knocked out two of my teeth and beat me until my eyes closed."

DR. CORNISH: Thank God you are now out of this cruel mess. I'm so sorry you went through such a brutal experience. Did you ever report him or have him arrested?

CAROL: No. He told me he would kill me. I was too afraid of him. No one knew. On the outside, I was always smiling. Everyone thought I was fine.

DR. CORNISH: Why didn't you tell anyone—someone?

CAROL: I was too ashamed. This is the first time I'm talking about it. You know, at one point I wanted to die. After a while I didn't care anymore—I didn't want to live like this anymore. I used to wish he would just kill me and get it over with.

BEWARE OF THE SELF-RIGHTEOUS WOLF IN SHEEP'S CLOTHING

DR. CORNISH: Why didn't you leave him sooner?

CAROL: He told me if I left him God would punish me.

DR. CORNISH: What?

CAROL: He would read and quote the Bible to me. He knew I believed in God and he used it to keep me with him. He would always repeat, "A woman is bound to her husband," and said we had to stick together "for better or worse, until death do we part."

DR. CORNISH: What a creep. He is the one who has a lot to answer to God for. Nowhere in the Bible does it say a woman must be battered by an abusive husband. But it does say, "Don't cast your pearls to swine." And he fits the role of a swine for the way he has brutalized you.

CAROL: He put me down so much that I used to believe him when he said that no other man would ever want me. If you saw him you would never believe he would do the things he did. A lot of times women would flirt with him, even in front of me. I would just say to myself, "If they only knew what I know." No one ever knows what happens behind closed doors.

DR. CORNISH: How did you get rid of him? Where is he now?

CAROL: *(Pause)* I think he's still in California. He used to go there for weeks at a time. The last time he left, I took our daughter and moved out. I just left everything. I'm living in an apartment rented under my cousin's name. And my phone number isn't listed. It has been four years and he doesn't know where I live. I am so happy to be alive today. I can't believe all the things I have accomplished since he's not around anymore—I have a good job, and I'm back in school studying for a degree in journalism. He always told me I wouldn't be anything. He was sure wrong!

DR. CORNISH: I know it took a lot of courage—good for you! I am so proud of you and happy for you. You should be so proud of yourself. Thank God he's yesterday's bad dream. Are you still legally married to him?

CAROL: Yes. But I use a different last name now.

DR. CORNISH: You should contact a lawyer and get a legal divorce from him. Ask if you can get an uncontested one on the grounds of abandonment. Let the lawyer know you are afraid of him, and you don't want him to know where you are. Get your divorce and erase all legal ties with him completely.

"MAYBE HE'LL CHANGE IN TIME" IS JUST WISHFUL THINKING UNLESS INTENSIVE THERAPY IS INVOLVED

Remember the familiar quote, "A leopard never changes his spots"? Well, this applies to the nature of human beings also. Unless one experiences a drastic situation or a spiritual awakening, people are basically set in their ways after the age of ten, when habits and patterns have already set in.

If you ever decide to look deep into your own behavioral pattern, you'll discover that who you are today is a result of early conditioning from your childhood family dynamics. Unless we develop the courage to create major turning points in our lives through self-analysis and honesty, we will be the same throughout our life spans.

Many sisters enter or remain in relationships with incompatible mates, hoping that their mates will change in time. The outcome is usually disastrous for both the man and woman involved.

Georgette is a thirty-five-year-old customer-service manager. She has been the victim of a bad marriage for over ten years. She is from a middle-class black family. She once was a very outgoing, energetic, and likable sister. When she met Troy at the age of twenty-four, her personality was altered.

She changed her lifestyle to live his. She readjusted her interests to incorporate his. She wanted to please him so much that she completely abandoned herself. She became another person—the one he wanted her to be.

THE HIGH PRICE OF AN EMOTIONALLY DANGEROUS LIAISON

A few years ago, Georgette and I were discussing how sisters often surrender against their will to suit their mates' demands. She shared, "Troy was insanely jealous. He abused me mentally. If I had male friends, he would accuse me of having affairs with them. That really hurt me, for he was the only man I wanted. Because his insecurities deepened, I severed all ties with my friends to please him. But this still wasn't enough for him. If a stranger looked at me, it made him jealous. So much so, he even went and slept with a prostitute. He confessed, crying, telling me he did it to 'get back at me.' I forgave him, assuring him that everything would be all right.

"There I was, consoling him, when I needed someone to soothe my pain. I was the one who was the victim. He was the unfaithful one—and with a hooker at that. I was hurting awfully bad. But I put my pain aside in order to comfort his. This is just one example of the hell I went through. I used to suffer from anxiety attacks because I was so unhappy."

DR. CORNISH: What kept you there for such a long time? Why did you continue to live in this misery?

GEORGETTE: The only way I can describe it is that it was like I was sitting by a well pumping for water. Every time I pulled the bucket up, it was empty, but I kept on pumping, and it kept coming up empty. I felt the minute I walked away, someone would come along, pump, and the bucket would overflow with water.

DR. CORNISH: When did you decide to get out of the situation?

GEORGETTE: Well, I decided to divorce him after our seventh year of marriage, but it took three more years to actually convince myself to go through with it. I still had hopes that he would change. I would express my hurts to him—the pain his actions caused me. His only response was "You'll get over it."

IF GIVEN ENOUGH TIME A SNAKE WILL EVENTUALLY UNCOIL ITSELF

"When he finally realized I was serious about leaving him, he told me that he wanted to make things work—that he loved me and didn't want to lose me. He said he wanted us to start a family. I got pregnant. He got worse. He took no interest in me. He moved into our other bedroom and looked at *Playboy* magazines and porn videos all night.

"He would be out practically every night visiting strip clubs until three, four, sometimes seven in the morning. My pregnancy was the loneliest time of my life. I was miserable, but I had to be strong for my baby. That's the only reason I got through the pregnancy.

"A few hours after our son was born, he came to visit me in the hospital. I'll never forget the words he said: 'Do you know where I can purchase a white-gold chain? I want to take my wedding ring off my finger and wear it around my neck instead.' The more I cried, the stronger I got. I realized I couldn't trust him with my feelings anymore. I had to take care of me."

CURE YOURSELF OF THE "DISEASE TO PLEASE"

"When I got out of the hospital, I told him, 'I won't let you hurt me anymore. I'm no longer the puppy you can abuse, who will always return to you for affection. You have changed me into a turtle. When you try to hurt me, I retreat into my shell, where you can't get to me, for protection.'

"I learned to turn within for strength. My marriage taught me what loneliness is. For the first time, I decided to do what was best for me. I wanted to be with him, but I needed my sanity. It wasn't as difficult as I imagined it would be. I was always afraid to do this, because I didn't want to be alone. Now that I think of it, he had given me plenty of practice being alone."

DR. CORNISH: What is the most important thing you think you'll take through life from this experience?

GEORGETTE: I have discovered that I am an important person. For the first time in a long time, I know what it's like to be me, and I like it.

"I WANT TO LEAVE HIM, BUT I CAN'T MAKE IT ON MY OWN"

A lot of sisters stay in disrespectful relationships because of economic entrapment. They feel that they are unable to make it out there on their own due to lack of adequate finances. Wilma is in her early sixties. She has been married for over thirty years now to a man who is an alcoholic. They have three children. Their marriage is one in name only. They have separate bedrooms. Wilma feels trapped and frustrated in her environment. She has always wanted a way out. She relates that she has always been miserable in her marriage.

One day while we were speaking about this sad relationship, I asked her why she remained in such an unhappy marriage. She responded, "I made the sacrifice for my children. I knew that if I went out on my own, I wouldn't be able to offer them the style of life I wanted them to have. It turned out I raised them by myself anyway, because their father was never home. He spent four days out of the week outside our home. He has another woman and two outside children. I worked both full- and part-time jobs to pay for my children's private schooling. Because I remained under his roof, I didn't have to worry about paying rent. It was hard enough trying to make ends meet with two jobs.

"The children are grown now and are doing well. Now that they are able to take care of themselves, it is time for me to take care of myself. They told me I should have left their abusive father years ago. I want to know what it's like to live just for me. I want to buy things I like, decorate a home the way I want to. I want to enjoy me. I'm leaving their father's house because he embarrasses me every time he drinks. If I had to do it again, I would have left him a long time ago."

As Long As You're Still Breathing You Can Make a New Choice

Wilma has made a thirty-year "sacrifice" because of her financial dependence. Although it relieved her slightly of economic burden, her marriage burdened her with thirty years of emotional grief. If you are in this predicament, what you must ask yourself is, "Is my financial security more important than my mental stability?"

Ten Excuses Women Make for Staying with an Abusive Mate

1. "He says he loves me."
2. "He says he didn't mean it."
3. "He says he's going through a hard time at work."

4. "He says he needs me to help him through this."
5. "He says he's trying to change."
6. "He says he wouldn't have done it if I didn't provoke him."
7. "He says no one understands him but me."
8. "He says he can't survive without me."
9. "He says he loses control when he is afraid of losing me."
10. "He says he's sorry and he won't do it again."

Forget about what he *says,* and pay attention to what he *does*. Remember, actions speak louder than words. To sum it all up: IF RESPECT HAS GONE, IT'S TIME TO MOVE ON!

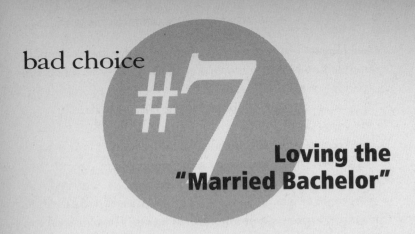

bad choice #7

Loving the "Married Bachelor"

I'm not going to pull any punches here: I cannot understand why any woman would settle for being a mere added appendage to a man who is already married. Let me warn you up front: I find infidelity inexcusable. And unless you are a young and confused teenager being manipulated by an unconscionable older married man, you won't find much pity from me here.

If you happen to be one of the sisters who is having an unscrupulous affair with another sister's husband, you may be a little disturbed by what I have to say here, and you may feel like hurling the book across the room. However, I strongly urge you to keep reading so you don't end up like one of these sisters whose stories I'm about to share with you.

IF YOU'RE STEALING LOVE ON THE SIDE, SOMEDAY YOU MAY GET LEFT ON THE OUTSIDE

You know, it always starts out the same. At first the affair with the married lover seems glamorous and enchanting. You may feel special that he's risking his family and reputation to steal a little love with you on the side. He promises he'll leave his wife someday. But as the years progress and you realize you will never be anything more to him than the side dish, you agonize.

Let's get straight to the point: It is pure fantasy to believe that you're going to find your true love married to another woman. It is common knowledge that men who cheat on their wives *always* cheat on their mistresses also.

This sister wrote to my column at the *New York Beacon*:

Dear Dr. Cornish:

I am a 44-year-old financially independent Black woman. I was married when I was nineteen years old and divorced by the time I was twenty-three. My husband, who was my first love, cheated on me. When he left so did my innocence and trust. Since then, I've dated married men. At first it was for revenge. I was so hurt that another woman took my husband, that I didn't care if I took another woman's man. Then it became a habit. One married man after the other. I figured if they would risk jeopardizing their marriage for me, then I must be worth it.

The reason I am writing to you is I've been seeing and supporting a married man for the past 11 years. He kept telling me he would leave his wife, but some excuse always kept him in the marriage. About two weeks ago, I found out I was not the only "other" woman in his life. And once again, I feel cheated on. I know this seems strange, but I really believed I was special, and I still want to be his wife. I really do love him, but I am not a 23-year-old now who can wait around until he makes up his mind to leave his wife, but I don't want to be alone. How can I get him to commit to only me?

D. B., Brooklyn, NY

STOP PLAYING MUSICAL CHAIRS WITH YOUR EMOTIONS

Dear D. B.:

As harsh as my answer may seem, it is for your own good. Snap out of it! Don't belittle yourself by settling for a part-time lover. Whoever said "ten percent of something is better than nothing at all" was not referring to a married man, I assure you.

Twenty years ago you were trusting and innocent and you were betrayed. As a result, you have experienced agonizing heartbreak. But two wrongs don't ever make it right. Many women who get involved with married men falsely believe that they are exclusive and become devastated when they find out otherwise. If a man can cheat on a woman he has taken a vow with, before God, believe me sis—he can cheat on you or anyone else.

Instead of worrying about him being committed to you, you must concentrate on *you* being committed to you. Commit to your self-acceptance and self-love. Being with a married man is depriving yourself of true joy. *You are playing "musical chairs" with your emotions. And, you are going to be the one left standing without a chair when the music stops.* Get out now! Don't look back!

Take at least six months before even thinking of getting involved again. In my book *Radiant Women of Color,* there is a healing chapter entitled "Know Thyself." It is a step-by-step guide which will help you to become more self-assured, embraceable and desirable.

With this new attitude, you can attract a single, decent and loving man who will desire you exclusively—but you must first believe that you deserve it.

SELF-DECEPTION IS THE BIGGEST LIE OF ALL

Thirty-seven-year-old Tiffany makes no bones about it when she volunteers, "I date only married men because I get more stuff out of them. Plus, I don't have the burden of a regular relationship. His wife is the one stuck with doing his laundry, cleaning the house, taking care of the kids, and all the dreary stuff. When he comes to see me we do fun things together. He helps to pay my bills and he leaves."

I wonder how long Tiffany will be reciting this code. I would like to hear from her three years from now. I've counseled too many women not to know that after a while, sooner or later, the act catches up to you. It's called laughing to keep from crying. Just like the words in Smokey Robinson's popular song "The Tears of a Clown": "Now if there's a smile on my face, it's only there tryin' to fool the public." I don't doubt that in the beginning you do believe that you are enjoying the situation. But as time progresses and he abandons you on enough weekends, holidays, and family vacations, you begin to see how empty your relationship with your part-time lover is. You start to want all the benefits the wife has. But you are afraid of speaking up because deep inside you know he would most likely just venture to another "added appendage" who is willing to play by his rules.

IF YOU GET THE "MARRIAGE" WARNING UP FRONT, WHY STEP FURTHER INTO THE DANGER ZONE?

It took forty-one-year-old Betty an entire decade to wake up to this truth about her triangular affair with her married bachelor. She met fifty-two-year-old Thomas, a mortgage broker, ten years ago when he came into her hair salon to have his hair trimmed. He was immediately attracted to her and became her weekly client. After the first two weeks of mutual flirting from the hairdresser's chair, they decided to take it to the dating stage. She had been divorced for nine years and had a ten-year-old daughter. He had been married for nineteen years and had a devoted wife and three teenage children—ages fourteen, sixteen, and eighteen.

HERE'S HOW THE LIE USUALLY BEGINS WHEN TRAVELING ON THE ROAD WHERE NO ONE WINS

Thomas told Betty he'd been having marital problems for years, but was staying in the relationship for their children's sake. He complained that his wife, an accountant, was too wrapped up in her work and had grown unresponsive and cold toward him sexually. He told Betty he found her irresistible and appealing and wished he had a wife like her. His flattery made her feel unique, and thus began their torrid long-term affair.

The first three years, they saw each other an average of three times per week. He was the only man she was seeing during this time. He would stay until late in the night at her apartment, but never slept over a full night, nor on weekends, because he didn't want his wife to become suspicious. Betty would never get to celebrate the holidays with him. But each time they were together he would tell her how much he loved her and that one day soon he would leave his wife and marry her. When she would ask him when he planned to fulfill his promise, he always told her he needed "a little more time until the kids were grown and on their own."

How Long Will It Take You to Discover There Are No Guarantees with a Part-Time Lover?

At the five-year mark, when his last child had left for college, Thomas's "little more time" went on for weeks, months and years before Betty admitted to herself that he was singing the same old song she had been listening to from day one.

Her daughter, now fifteen, had become very attached to Thomas and by now was questioning her mother about why he hadn't ever married her. Betty became fed up and frustrated at Thomas's five-year stall and confronted him about this since his children were all grown and out of the house. As usual, he asked for an extended time period. After three months, and no more valid excuses, she gave him an ultimatum. He didn't take to that very well at all. He walked out. She didn't hear from him for weeks, but decided that since she had invested five years of her life in him, she wasn't going to give up—she wanted him to fulfill his promise and make her his wife.

DESPERATE NEEDS LEAD TO DESPERATE DEEDS

Betty became desperate. She made up her mind to do everything to win him over. The first thing she decided to do was to discreetly check out his wife. In her words, she wanted to see "what the competition looked like." She had seen pictures of her in the past, but she wanted to see her face-to-face and sum her up. She knew where his wife's office was. She used an assumed name, had fake business cards printed with a voice-mail number and a post-office box, and pretended she needed an accountant for her new business. She made an appointment to see Thomas's wife and had a half-hour meeting about the accounting services she could provide. After the meeting, Betty excused herself and told the accountant she would be contacting her soon.

PITFALLS, POTHOLES, AND EVEN DEEPER DITCHES . . .

Betty couldn't wait to go outside to give herself a thumbs-up for her trickery and discovery. In her mind, she believed she was much more attractive than Thomas's wife, and she should have no problem winning him over. This strengthened her mission to get Thomas to commit to her. She figured she would wine him, dine him, and seduce him. She called Thomas and apologized to him for giving him an ultimatum. She invited him to have dinner at her home. He readily accepted, and she sent her daughter to her sister's home for the evening. When Thomas arrived, Betty greeted him in sheer lingerie. A delicious candlelit dinner and a bottle of expensive champagne awaited him. For the first time in their five years together, he spent the entire night at her home.

IF YOU ARE WAITING IN VAIN YOU'LL EVENTUALLY BE LEFT WITH HEARTBREAK AND PAIN

This gave Betty hope that she was moving closer to becoming the "new wife" in his life. However, when she came to seek advice from me, another five years had already slipped by. Betty decided to get off this carousel ride.

BETTY: My daughter—she got involved with a young man I wouldn't have chosen for her. She got pregnant and they went to the justice of the peace and got married behind my back because she knew I didn't approve of him. When I found out and confronted her, she retaliated by saying, "Ma, at least he loves me enough to marry me. You are living a lie with Thomas. He's never going to marry you. He has used you all these years. And as long as you let him, you'll be nothing but a mistress to him." She spelled out to me what I was afraid of seeing. I think it's time to move on.

DR. CORNISH: "Out of the mouths of babes." Betty, it's always a no-win situation to get involved with a married man. All the guy is doing is playing house on the side and lying to both women involved. You knew that he was married from the start. But he sold you the hope of lies. And you bought into it for ten long years. You wasted a whole decade of your life plotting to get somebody else's man, when you could have been building a life with a productive partner of your own. Do you really want this married man?

BETTY: Yes . . . No. I'm not sure anymore. No.

DR. CORNISH: This will answer it for you. If you should get married to this man tomorrow, would you be able to sleep peacefully at night knowing that you can trust him, or would you live in constant turmoil, wondering who he's with every time he tells you he has to work late?

BETTY: I would never trust him. He has called his wife from my bed often, telling her he's caught up with a client.

DR. CORNISH: And you lay there snuggled up with him while he lied to that unsuspecting sister . . . pretend it was your daughter's husband doing that to her.

BETTY: No. I couldn't bear it. I would never want anyone to do that to her.

DR. CORNISH: So, what are you going to do?
BETTY: It's over for good this time.

THE THRILL AND THE KILL CAN BE EQUALLY DANGEROUS

Betty finally left Thomas after she realized she was hanging on in vain. I wish more women would understand that the initial "thrill" they get from believing they can "steal somebody else's guy" is the same emotional dagger that will "kill" their own relationship in the long run.

After a two-year affair, thirty-four-year-old Lillian finally got her married lover to get a divorce from his young wife and four-month-old baby. Lillian had caused the young sister a lot of pain, and even bluntly declared during a confrontation, "If you had what it took to please him, he wouldn't have come looking for me." But two kids and eight years later—surprise! Lillian is heartbroken and bitter to find out that for three years he has been having a relationship with a coworker.

Well, Lillian, how did you get this husband of yours in the first place? Maybe you can go back to the young sister who was his first wife to ask for coping skills in how to deal with a cheating, good-for-nothing, runabout mate.

WHY TRY TO GAIN BY ANOTHER SISTER'S PAIN?

I remember when, after taping an episode of *Ricki Lake* called "I Say Your Man Is Fair Game; Watch Out, Girl, I'm on a Mission," my service received numerous calls from women seeking advice. I'll share a few of their stories here with you. One of the most heartrending cases was that of thirty-seven-year-old Claudette.

My assistant had originally scheduled Claudette's appointment for two weeks after she called. But she kept calling, three times each day, to ask if I would see her right away. Because of the urgency in her voice, we rescheduled her a week early. The moment Claudette walked through the door, she was in tears. She said she had nowhere to turn and no one to confide in, and she had seen how straightforward I was on the show and hoped I could give her some comfort and direction. Here's her story:

Claudette and her thirty-nine-year-old husband, Norris, are originally from the Caribbean. He was her first love and is the only man she has ever been with. They have been married for seventeen years and have a thirteen- and a fourteen-year-old son. Norris cheated on Claudette a few times in the past, back in their homeland. They migrated to the United States a little over fifteen years ago. Claudette explained that they originally got their alien registration cards through an immigration lawyer but later found out that he was crooked and the cards were invalid. The government took the cards away, but since they have a legitimate printing business and have been paying taxes for the past twelve years, they have not been deported yet. Both of their sons are American citizens.

"If It Looks Like a Snake, It Probably Is"

Claudette works in the printing shop with Norris. She works an average of ten to twelve hours each day. They used to work side by side, but for the past eighteen months, Norris has been leaving her in the shop by herself to run things, and coming home in the wee hours of the morning. At first, whenever she confronted him he would either become hostile, or walk out on her.

Claudette believed that Norris was cheating, but she had no concrete evidence. He kept telling her that she was imagining things—that it was only in her mind, and that she was going crazy.

"The Proof Is in the Pudding"

But during the following year, his reckless behavior intensified. Whenever the phone rang at home, he would rush to answer it and either conduct his conversations in a stilted manner or go into another room to continue. He would leave shortly after the conversations, declaring he was going to hang out with some of "the guys." Norris, who had always been the casual T-shirt-and-jeans type of man, started dressing up and buying expensive cologne. His sexual interest in Claudette dwindled, and he kept attacking her appearance. But the more she insisted he was cheating, the more he insisted that she was going crazy.

NEVER DOUBT YOUR FEMININE INTUITION

After a year of this behavior, Claudette really felt as if she was going crazy with grief. She felt as if she was on the verge of a nervous breakdown. Norris saw her discomfort and misery, but kept insisting that she was hallucinating. Sometimes she found herself crying, walking, and talking to herself on the street, and she realized she was falling apart and had to get an answer.

There were four male workers in the printing shop, all buddies of Norris. All of them knew his secrets. She sensed this, but none of them would talk to her about it. She felt ashamed and embarrassed to go into the shop, but she had a responsibility to make the business work for her husband. So every day she would bear the pain silently, knowing that they all knew.

One Saturday afternoon she decided to pay a visit to Winsome, the wife of one of Norris's pals from the shop. She knew that this sister enjoyed community gossip and that if anyone knew the truth, she would. She also knew that this woman wouldn't readily surrender information, because Norris was her husband's boss, so Claudette decided to trick it out of her.

When Claudette got to Winsome's house she put on a brave face and told a falsehood—she told Winsome that she'd just gone through a bad time with Norris, but that he had finally told her the truth about his affair. They were getting a separation, but she had to be strong for her kids. That's all she needed to say before Winsome took the ball and ran with it: "Claudette, I told them I didn't want that slackness in my house. I'm glad he finally told you the truth. He kept bringing the girl here on the weekends. He and the fellows would play dominoes and drink white rum and beer in the backyard, while she sat around making conversation with the rest of the women. I knew it wasn't right, but my husband warned me to mind my own business."

THE AGONY OF DECEIT

Claudette's worst nightmare had been confirmed. She sat quietly with her insides churning in agony, as Winsome gave her the mistress's profile, including her address and phone number. Claudette recognized that this was one of the women Norris had fooled around with some years ago, back in the Caribbean.

When she left, she kept up the brave front and thanked Winsome for the information. But as soon as she got outside, she bawled like a newborn baby needing comfort at her mother's bosom. She had no one to nurture her—no friend's shoulder to lean on. But as awkward as it may seem, she was somewhat relieved to have her suspicions confirmed, because now she knew for sure that she wasn't "crazy," as Norris had so often accused.

Claudette went to the mistress's house in rage. She wasn't there, but her elderly mother answered the door. In tears, Claudette shared her dilemma with her and asked her to make her daughter stop interfering with her family life. The mother was compassionate to Claudette's trauma, but said, "I didn't raise her to be this way. But she's a grown woman now and makes her own decisions. And besides, Norris told me he had been divorced from you for two years now."

WHEN HE'S THIS DESPICABLE, IT'S TIME TO STOP SHACKING, AND SEND HIM PACKING

When Claudette confronted Norris that evening, he avoided giving her a straight answer and wanted to know how she had gotten the mistress's address. After all of that, he still denied the affair and told Claudette that he was ashamed of her for not trusting him and for going behind his back to snoop. He insisted they were only "good friends."

Norris dismissed any further communication about the subject of his infidelity, and for the following eight months he continued his escapades. And he still continued to tell Claudette that she was overreacting about his "good friend." Claudette endured this mess because she didn't want her marriage to end.

Five weeks before Claudette contacted me, Norris asked her for a "temporary divorce" so he could get married to his "good friend" "for immigration purposes only." He claimed that because she was such a "good friend" and was a legal resident of the United States, she was willing to marry him so that he could file for legal permanent residency. He told Claudette that after he received his alien registration card, he would divorce his "good friend" and remarry Claudette, then file for Claudette's permanent residency.

IF YOU'RE BEING TAKEN FOR A RIDE, ALWAYS GET A GOOD LAWYER ON YOUR SIDE

By the time she spoke with me, Claudette had endured as much as she could take in this dishonest marriage. Claudette cried nonstop throughout our entire conversation.

CLAUDETTE: I just want some peace and quiet. If it weren't for my kids, I'd just disappear. I've given him everything and he tried to make me think I was crazy all this time. I helped him to build our business and now he wants me to give him a divorce to marry her for a green card.

DR. CORNISH: Claudette, I think the first thing you have to do is realize you are worth much more than this. I will help you to work on that. But you also need to get a legitimate immigration attorney to get your legal residence status straightened out.

CLAUDETTE: I don't have the amount of money lawyers ask for. He controls the business and everything is in his name.

DR. CORNISH: This is a common mistake that too many married women make too often. You trust all your finances in your husband's name, and he controls them. Since you have no financial power in the business, your husband should be paying you as a salaried employee.

You need to have your own bank account and establish some sort of credit in your name. If he should walk out on you tomorrow, you would have nothing to show for all those years of marriage and working. As far as the immigration lawyer is concerned, you can contact legal aid for free information.

"Expect the Unexpected"

I gave Claudette some positive affirmations and reading materials to build up her self-esteem. She had surrendered her individuality to her husband and had become his shadow. No woman ever wants to believe that her marriage may end, but just in case serious problems occur, you should always have your own money set aside so you'll always be in control of whether you stay and try to work things out or choose to leave.

What a Cruel Plate to Have Dished Out to You!

More often than not, women who get involved with married men know from the beginning, or somewhere in the early stages of the affair, that the man is already spoken for. But there are quite a few cases where men have blatantly lied for months and even years about their marital status.

The episode of *Ricki Lake* that prompted Claudette's call motivated another caller to share this: Kim, a twenty-two-year-old college student, said she had been seeing thirty-year-old

Claude, a mechanical engineer, for four years. She had just found out during the previous summer that he had been married for five years and had a four-year-old daughter and a two-year-old son. She didn't know what to do. She loved and hated him at the same time. He had been her first love. She was living with her mother, but for the past four years she had spent a lot of time at his home, which he shared with his sister.

Claude was always attentive to and available for Kim. She had no reason to suspect that he was cheating. However, he and his sister had a major falling-out, and out of revenge, his sister decided to tell Kim the truth at last. When Kim accused her of lying she took Kim to a second house that Claude owned and introduced her to his wife and kids.

"Drop Him Like a Hot Potato!"

Kim thought she was in the midst of a cruel nightmare. However, the wicked reality hit when she confronted Claude. He told her that he was sorry, but he hadn't told her about his family in the beginning because he had known she wouldn't have dated him, and he had been afraid of telling her later because he hadn't wanted to lose her. She didn't know what to do, but then decided to leave him. But after weeks of grieving and being flooded by his apologies, they resumed an on-again, off-again relationship.

Kim told me that she was very confused about her feelings for Claude, saying, "I hate him for what he has done, but part of me still loves him." Her confusion was understandable. She was an innocent victim in this defeating love triangle. I sympathized with her and asked her if she believed it was in her best interest to share herself with a man who lied to her and tricked her. When she answered no, I told her that even though she loved Claude, she had to love herself more and not be used like this. "It's best to sever all ties with him and start from scratch," I continued. "It's going to take a while before you can trust again, but you still have your whole life ahead of you. You deserve a better man." Kim agreed and made the smart decision to leave this unbalanced relationship.

Sisters indulging in man-sharing frequently ask me how to get the man to commit to them. My response is always the same: Never settle for a part-time man. This is a no-win situation. If you find out he's already married, engaged, or committed, drop him like a hot potato!

THE DECEITFUL DOUBLE STANDARD

Do you know that some men will put their wives on pedestals at home, expecting them to act saintly, but go scouting around for unconventional sex with other women whom they use for sexual experimentation? It's called the *"Madonna-whore complex."* The men view their wives as a "nice girls" who shouldn't indulge in gratifying sex. If their wives initiate sex that is outside of their idea of the norm, some of these brothers will chastise them for being unladylike, yet they sneak around with mistresses to fulfill their lust. Talk about a double standard!

IF YOU HAVE CHOSEN TO BE PART OF HIS OUTSIDE LIFE, WHY GET JEALOUS BECAUSE YOU'RE NOT HIS WIFE?

Twenty-seven-year-old Jade boasts of herself as a "professional mistress." For the past six years, she has dated one married man after the next. According to Jade, her past lovers, like her current one, forty-seven-year-old Bill, have tried things with her that they are too rigid to do with their wives at home.

Jade says she feels a sense of "power" when she gets Bill to fulfill his wildest dreams. However, she confesses that she often feels angry or jealous of the protective feelings he has for his wife. One afternoon while he was licking her toes, Jade playfully looked down at Bill and asked, "What would your wife say if she saw you sucking my toes? What would you say if your wife had someone doing hers while you are here doing mine?" In a rage, Bill sprang to his feet and screamed, "You leave my wife out of this." He got dressed and left.

IF YOU CHEAPEN YOURSELF, YOU WILL BE TREATED CHEAPLY

After a couple of days Jade and Bill gravitated back to each other. However, Jade contacted me at the end of January after seeing me appear on *Ricki Lake*. She called to vent her anger about Bill.

JADE: He uses my body to do the things he can't do with his wife. I do it all with him. And you know what he bought me for Christmas? A cheap fifty-dollar pair of gold hoop earrings. You know what he bought her? A diamond tennis bracelet for almost three thousand dollars! And he asked me if I thought she would like it—can you believe this?

DR. CORNISH: What did you tell him when he asked your opinion about his wife's gift?

JADE: I told him off.

DR. CORNISH: Why?

JADE: Because I'm worth more than that cheap cheesy gift he gave me. I told him I should have gotten the diamonds and that stuck-up boring woman he's married to should have gotten the flimsy-ass gold hoops.

DR. CORNISH: What did he do?

JADE: He told me not to talk about her like that because I wasn't fit to walk in her shoes. Then I got pissed and slapped him. He walked out, but then called me back a few days later.

DR. CORNISH: Are you still seeing him?

JADE: Yes. But I'm still pissed at him.

DR. CORNISH: You need to stop seeing this married man. You're putting a price on your sexuality. And he's only using you as a sperm deposit. He has no respect for you. Why belittle yourself like this?

As our conversation continued, Jade became aware of how damaged her self-image was. I pointed out that Bill had bought her the "cheap" gift because in his mind that's all he thought she was worth. I made it clear that although Bill was a dishonest and disrespectful married man, she was responsible for the perception he had of her because she marketed herself as a "professional mistress." Bill was only fitting into the self-defeating pattern she had created for herself, and if it hadn't been him, it would have been some other married man.

"The real issue should not be about Bill's present," I observed, "but about his presence in you life. Why are you dating a married guy?"

Under my prodding, Jade admitted that her father had always cheated on her mother. She said her father's affairs had caused her mother to become an alcoholic. So she had made a childhood promise to herself that she would never get married. She was conditioned to believe that the mistress had the power over the wife.

I helped Jade to realize that there was no power in soliciting someone else's husband. The real power was in freeing herself of negative childhood memories, developing her self-worth, and creating a respectable life for herself.

At the close of our talk, Jade agreed to leave Bill and work on redefining her goals and establishing a better lifestyle for herself.

THERE IS NO PRIZE IN MAN-SHARING

Often sisters are looking for an easy way in life and believe that being involved with a married man will provide a hassle-free relationship. As I mentioned earlier, getting involved with a man who has already taken a vow with another sister is always a no-win situation. I'm still unsure why sisters would settle for man-sharing. Whatever their individual reasons, I hope you realize that you deserve to have a worthwhile man of your own.

Would you want to end up being stuck in perpetual limbo with a married man like this?

Dear Dr. Cornish:

I have been married for 22 years to my wife. I was 21 and she was 18. We have four daughters together, ages 15 to 21. I have always wanted a son. We kept trying, but after the birth of our fourth girl, we decided my wife would have her tubes tied. Many of my male coworkers have sons and often boast about their father-son bonding, which makes me feel depressed about not having a son.

A female coworker and I had become good friends and she tried to cheer me up by telling me not to be so hard on myself. She started flirting with me and told me there was nothing wrong with me. I was not the reason my wife didn't have a boy, it was entirely her [the wife's] fault. She joked and said if it were her who was pregnant, she would give me the son she knew I wanted so badly. We eventually did become intimate and she became pregnant and she did have the son my wife was unable to give me. I will always love her for that. My son is now 13 years old.

My situation is that I love both women for different reasons. I will never leave either of them. Women may not understand this, but it is possible for a man to love two women at the same time. It does get confusing sometimes, and on many days it's hard to keep my feelings straight. I work long and tiring hours and don't want to be nagged when I get home. My wife is still very angry with me after all these years. I love her and will never leave her, but when she starts an argument, I just leave the house and go to my son's mother's home. Why don't women realize that when they nag their man all they are doing is forcing him into another woman's arms?

L. F., Brooklyn, NY

IS THIS BROTHER FOR REAL?

Dear L. F.:

It's quite understandable that a man would want a son to carry on his name. Men see themselves in their boys, as women see themselves in their daughters. It's natural for you to want a father-son bonding. However, your information and reasoning were way off base. It is certainly no one's "fault" whether a boy or girl is the gender of the offspring. Where were you during biology classes when we were taught that it is the male gene which most often determines the sex of the child? All female bodies have only the X chromosome while the male carries both the X and Y. During mating if the male ejects an X which meets with one of the female's X's then a girl is produced. In any case, each child, regardless of its sex, should be considered a blessing.

It was simply a matter of timing, nothing more, nothing less. Your mistress at work tricked you. She had a 50/50 chance just as your wife did. It was only by chance that your body produced the Y gene at the time you mated. If you were perhaps just a little more patient, it could have been your wife that you would have shared that gene with, and your messy situation would have been avoided.

In answer to your question as to why women nag cheating men, it is forgivable if one makes a mistake, but you seem to take pride in your dual lifestyle. I completely agree with you that your wife shouldn't nag you. I believe she should *leave* you. You should consider yourself lucky that she has put up with your infidelity. It's people like you who make the label "wrong and strong." Even though you are the one who did the wrong, you are strongly opposed to your wife voicing her opinion on the pain and betrayal she feels. Wouldn't it be something if marriage vows included the following toast: "Here's to me, here's to you, here's to love and laughter, I'll be true as long as you, and not a single moment after"? Put yourself in her position. How would you react to having to share your wife with another man?

DON'T BECOME A PAWN IN A TRIANGLE OF PAIN

I quite agree that people grow apart. And if both parties don't grow together, one will outgrow the other. Then divorce or separation is the best solution. That isn't the issue here. The issue is about the lying and cheating that leads to pain and hurt.

Do you know what I do when I am approached by married bachelors? First, I give them the "You have got to be joking" look; then, I bluntly ask them, "What if your wife was out trying to solicit an outside love interest the same way you are trying to make a pass at me now?" The semidecent ones always get the initial guilty look, like a little boy caught with his hand in the cookie jar; then they get the embarrassed look (as they should); then they bow out gently and leave. (I say semidecent, because the decent married ones would not be out hunting in the first place.)

However, the unscrupulous ones just make some ridiculous comment and move on to the next target. These are the walking robots who have developed the master craftsmanship of lying— and will tell you anything to get laid on the side. Don't fall for it, sis.

Do any of these sound familiar?

THE TEN LIES MOST FREQUENTLY USED BY "MARRIED BACHELORS"

1. "My wife has let her body go. She gained too much weight after the births of our children. She doesn't take care of herself anymore."

2. "My wife is boring in bed. She doesn't want to try anything new. She doesn't like to have sex anymore. She doesn't turn me on anymore."

3. "My wife is too involved in her career (or the kids). She doesn't make time for me anymore."

4. "My wife doesn't understand me. She is cold and bitter. All she does is argue, criticize, and nag me all the time."

5. "My wife cheated on me. And now I can't trust her anymore. I just can't be the faithful husband to her anymore."

6. "My wife says that if I leave, either she'll commit suicide or she'll find me and kill me."

7. "My wife is holding up the divorce. She says if I go through with it, I'll never see my kids again."

8. "My wife has a terminal illness. I cannot leave her right now, but we are no longer having sex."

9. "My wife should be just like you. She could learn a lot from you. I wish I had met you before I got married. You would be the perfect wife for me."

10. "My wife . . . what wife? That was my sister's voice you heard in the background."

FACE YOURSELF BEFORE YOU DISGRACE YOURSELF

It's always the wife's fault, huh? How would you feel if you were the wife being bashed like this? You just may be someday—so be careful where you step, because whatever road you're paving now, you're going to have to walk on someday.

Instead of being flattered by these ridiculous utterances, gather your self-respect together and send the fibbing fellow home to his wife—where he belongs!

bad choice

#8

Emotional Dependency Plus Unplanned Pregnancy

Children are very precious. It takes a lot of responsibility, sacrifice, and love to raise healthy-minded children. Unfortunately, many sisters have neglected to think of this at the time of conception. Some share that their pregnancies resulted from being caught up in the moment of passion. Others claim that the condom broke. Still others lament, "He promised we would always be together."

If the relationship is not built on solid ground from the beginning, the promise of togetherness is abruptly broken the minute the pregnancy test reads "positive." The "sperm donor" does a Houdini act and magically disappears into thin air.

Truth be told, there are many sisters who use pregnancy as a tool, attempting to entrap their lovers into forced marriages. And when it backfires, they are heartbroken.

IF YOUR LOVE HAS GONE BAD, JUST BE TRUE, AND DON'T TRY TO USE A BABY LIKE KRAZY GLUE

If you're in an unproductive relationship, face up to it. Get rid of it, and move on. A baby is not to be used as glue to hold a broken relationship together.

This sister wrote to the *New York Beacon,* seeking my advice:

Dear Dr. Cornish:

I am a single, 30-year-old, never-married (no kids), intelligent, professional, pretty dark-skinned Black woman. I've been deeply involved with a handsome, 32-year-old, light-skinned Black man for the past five years.

We are both in love with each other; the problem is his family. Although they are very polite to me on the surface, they are very much against our relationship.

He told me that his parents told him they want him to marry "someone more like them." When I asked him what that meant, he said they mean someone "light-skinned." They are all so light-skinned, they can pass for white.

They are an extremely close family and though they claim to be very proud of their Black heritage, I guess it's not enough to accept my dark skin as part of the family.

I am very hurt and torn apart over this. I didn't fall in love with the man because of his complexion. I fell in love with the way he treated me. *He keeps telling me he wants us to get married, but he wants me to get pregnant first. When I asked him why, he says that he knows his family would accept me if I was going to have his baby.*

I am really confused. I don't know what to do. I love him but I can't let this destroy me. I don't know what to do; maybe you can write me and give me some advice.

M. R., White Plains, NY

FACE REALITY—A CHILD CANNOT BE YOUR "EMOTIONAL ELIXIR" OR YOUR "RELATIONSHIP FIXER"

Dear M. R.:

It's easy to understand your confusion and pain. African-Americans have struggled long and hard trying to rise above discrimination from other ethnic groups, we certainly don't need to have it within our own race.

It's very sad that some Blacks, dark and light, are caught up in that kind of prejudice that only brings division, when we need to embrace each other's beauty and contributions.

If your lover's family does not accept you because of your skin coloring, then let that be their problem and not yours. If your mate is not mature enough to stand up to his family in defense of the love he supposedly has for you, then you don't need him.

Total love is accepting the entire package. *If he needs a baby as an excuse to marry, then he is doing both of you a great disservice. You have given this man five years of your life already and you know what his family thinks of you—what's next? If your baby is born dark, then both of you will experience the pain and rejection from his family.*

Letting go of a relationship is difficult. It is probably one of the hardest emotional roller coasters we will ride. But what's even harder is the hurt one lives with when it is a mismatched union.

It's time to move on and free yourself of him and his narrow-minded family. After you free yourself, you can heal and find someone who will appreciate you for who you are and will admire the beauty in the darkness of your skin.

IF PREGNANCY HAS YOU IN DISTRESS, A SHOTGUN WEDDING WON'T SOLVE YOUR MESS

Using a baby as an escape from dealing with the real problems in a relationship will only end up harming the child. If the relationship is not compatible from the beginning, there is no way a child will keep it together. I sincerely hope this sister took my advice and refrained from bringing a child into that unhealthy environment. If not, she may end up in a situation like that of a couple I counseled on an episode of *Tempestt* entitled "We Had the Baby; Now I Want a Divorce."

During this episode, three couples confessed that they had

used pregnancy as an excuse to try to keep their relationships together. Two of the couples said they were forced into their marriages by their parents. One of the young men on stage said he felt the shotgun marriage was "forced down his throat" because of the pregnancy, and that he and his wife had started having severe problems just one month after they were married.

Nineteen-year-old Maxine admitted to getting pregnant because twenty-year-old Leonard talked her into it. He no longer wanted anything to do with her. She shared this: "He was such a sweetheart at first. We decided to get pregnant, but he would always change his mind at the last minute. When we finally got pregnant, his mother decided we should get married, because we didn't have a place to stay. After we got married, I had a miscarriage, and it got quiet between us. Then he decided we should have another baby right away. We tried, and after a week and a half, I got pregnant again."

She revealed that Leonard had been cheating on her before their baby was born. And, now his cheating had gotten worse. He had not taken an active role as a father to their baby. She said, "All he does is sleep around with different women. He only comes to see me when he wants money and sex."

Leonard was very hostile to Maxine onstage. He openly declared that he didn't want anything to do with her and wished she would just move on with her life.

YOU'VE GOT TO LEARN TO LIKE EACH OTHER BEFORE YOU CAN GROW TO LOVE EACH OTHER

The men in the first two couples wanted to end their relationships. The women said they wanted to work things out because they were still in love with the men. After a commercial break the host asked me if divorce was the answer to the problems the couples were facing. I said it depended on whether or not the couples could reach a compatible agreement where they could get along and genuinely *like* each other as friends; then their relationships would have a chance. But if they couldn't learn to listen and communicate with each other, and one person definitely wanted out, then the best thing to do was to separate.

As the show progressed, Maxine continued pleading with Leonard to try to works things out. He became more hostile and said that the child would always bond them together, but that he "definitely wanted out of the marriage" because he wasn't in love with her. This inspired a vicious and heated argument between them, and they both admitted to the practice of physically abusing each other.

"You two must deal with the best interest of the child," I interrupted. "It's an ideal situation for a child to have an environment where there are two parents, but it is damaging for a child to see two parents who cannot even speak to each other in a civil manner." They listened as I continued, "You two were thrown into a marriage. Your parents thought they were doing the right thing at the time. But you did not learn to *like* each other—just to *like* each other as friends first. That's past and gone. Let's deal with the best interest of the child now."

Maxine was deeply hurt by Leonard's decision to divorce, but she agreed to "try" to form a civilized friendship with him for their child's sake.

THIS MENTALITY HAS GOT TO GO!

I can't understand how any woman would try to keep a man from seeing his child from a previous relationship. That's pure selfishness—especially with black men having such a bad rap for abandoning their kids (and a lot of them do). It's refreshing to see a brother who takes full responsibility for the offspring he helped bring into this world. Any sister who would demand that a man not take responsibility for any of his children, regardless of his current status, is backward and ridiculous.

Shaquanna, twenty-three, is an example of someone with this mentality. I counseled her when she appeared on *Ricki Lake*. She was opposed to her husband having anything to do with his three-year-old daughter, Gabrielle, from a previous relationship. Her husband, twenty-five-year-old Aaron, said that before they were married Shaquanna had led him to believe that she accepted Gabrielle. But as soon as they crossed the threshold, he had begun to feel tricked because Shaquanna refused to accept his daughter.

He said that he had believed that once they had a child of their own, things would improve. But instead, it had gotten worse since Shaquanna had given birth to their daughter. And now she was insisting that he choose between the two girls.

Aaron brought his wife on the show because he wanted to make a plea to save their marriage. Their Thanksgiving holiday had been spent apart because Shaquanna had refused to have little Gabrielle around. Shaquanna had taken their daughter to her mother's house and Aaron had taken Gabrielle to his mother's house for dinner. He wanted Shaquanna to accept Gabrielle and for them to spend the Christmas holiday as a family.

Aaron told Shaquanna that he loved her "with all his heart." "But," he said, "this problem we're having about Gabrielle is killing our marriage. And I don't want that to happen. I just want us to be happy. I want you to accept her."

Onstage Shaquanna reluctantly agreed to accept Gabrielle as part of the immediate family. She smiled and said, "I don't know. I'll give it a try. That's all I can say; I'll try it. I do have a hard time, though, but I'm going to try."

WHY BLAME AN INNOCENT CHILD FOR YOUR INSECURITIES?

When the taping of the show was over, Shaquanna stormed off the stage and threw a temper tantrum in the greenroom. She was angry at Aaron and accused him of "bringing her on national TV to embarrass her." One of the producers asked me if I would speak to her before I left. Aaron stood attentively by her side during our conversation.

DR. CORNISH: Shaquanna, why are you upset? You seemed fine onstage.

SHAQUANNA: I didn't want to say anything out there because I didn't want the audience to embarrass me. But he knows I don't like his other daughter.

DR. CORNISH: Why don't you like her?

SHAQUANNA: I don't know. It's not her, really. It's her mother that I can't stand.

DR. CORNISH: The little girl is innocent. She is only a three-year-old child. Whatever differences you have with the mother have nothing to do with the child. That's your husband's daughter. He had her before he even met you. It's unfair of you to demand that he choose.

SHAQUANNA: I just don't like her. I don't like seeing her. Now he brought me out here on TV, and her mother is going to see the show, and probably laugh at me because he said I'm killing our marriage.

DR. CORNISH: Why are you concerned about what Gabrielle's mother thinks? She isn't the issue. Forget about her. But you'd better pay attention to what your husband feels. If you don't stop campaigning against his daughter, all you're going to do is drive him away from you. Then you'll really give Gabrielle's mother something to laugh about. *(To Aaron)* Why is she so upset about this woman? Have you given her reasons to be?

AARON: *(Compassionately)* No. I broke up with her two years before I even met Shaquanna. Shaquanna knows there's nothing going on. She knows I love only her, and I don't want to lose her. But my daughter is part of my heart.

WHY BLOCK A BROTHER FROM DOING THE RIGHT THING?

DR. CORNISH: *(To Aaron)* I'm so proud of you for taking such responsibility and not abandoning your child. Shaquanna, you have a decent man. You should be glad he's the way he is. What if your dislike for his daughter drives him away? Would you want him to neglect the daughter he has with you?

SHAQUANNA: *(Reluctantly)* No.

DR. CORNISH: You wouldn't want that for your child, so why should you wish that on another child? Think about this, Shaquanna—what if you got divorced and ended up with another man who told you he didn't want your child from a previous relationship around? What would you do?

SHAQUANNA: *(Lashing out angrily)* I'd tell him to go to hell . . . that's my baby! I wouldn't let any man come between me and my child, no matter how much I might love him.

DR. CORNISH: That's precisely how your husband feels. Now, do you understand the magnitude of what you're demanding? Put yourself in his shoes. What would you do?

ALL CHILDREN DESERVE TO BE LOVED

SHAQUANNA: I wouldn't want him to turn his back on our baby. I guess it's not right for me to ask him to do that to Gabrielle. She really didn't do anything to me. It's just . . . *(Pause)*

DR. CORNISH: It's just that you love him so much and you're jealous that his daughter might take up too much of his time. *(Smile)* Right?

SHAQUANNA: *(Smiling)* Ye . . . Yeah. *(Aaron embraces her)*

DR. CORNISH: *(Smiling)* My dear, you've got a good man. Love him and love his daughter. Look at her as an extension of your husband. Treat her kindly—let your daughter grow up around her sister. There are too many broken black families out there. You are a beautiful young couple. I know you can work this out. Look at how much he loves you. *(Aaron smiles affectionately at her)* Don't drive him away. Form a strong team and work together. How about it, Shaquanna?

SHAQUANNA: *(Laughs)* Yep! I will. *(To Aaron)* I'm sorry, baby. I love you. We'll work it out.

This is why I do what I do. I enjoy helping people to bring out the best in their individual situations. The solutions may not always be perfect, but they're always practical. While we're on the subject of practical solutions, let's take a look at the following letter a sister wrote to my advice column at the *New York Beacon*:

LEARN TO MAKE THE BEST OF THE WORST FOR YOUR CHILD'S SAKE

Dear Dr. Cornish:

I am a 38-year-old successful Black woman. Seven years ago, while trying to get over the breakup of a long-term relationship, I had a summer romance with someone whom I thought was an honest 34-year-old professional Black man. I was very heartbroken at the time and he was attentive and passionate.

Within the first month he asked me to marry him. I said yes. We had sex and I became pregnant. When I told him I was pregnant, he told me to have an abortion and not to ever call him again. Then, I found out he was already married to one woman, living with another, and had also gotten another woman pregnant.

The entire revelation was completely overwhelming, but I didn't believe in abortion and decided to have the baby for me. I went through the pregnancy by myself and after my child was born, I called him to let him know. He said he didn't care, and to go on with my life and leave him alone. I did just that. I became very well-adjusted, successful and independent. Four years ago I got married to a genuinely supportive and wealthy man, who has adopted my child, and is raising my child as his own.

The problem is the estranged "summer fling" of seven years ago now wants to publicly declare himself the father of my child and has the nerve to demand visitation rights. I don't want him anywhere near my child. It's not out of anger or revenge, but there's simply no purposeful place for him in our lives. Some of my family members seem to think I'm wrong and insist that "a child should have the right to know its natural parent, no matter what." I'm not writing about the legal aspect of this; I'm more concerned about the moral issue. What is your advice?

M. H., New York, NY

THERE IS A MAJOR DIFFERENCE BETWEEN A "DADDY" AND A "SPERM DONOR"

Dear M. H.:

Morally, you are right on target! Don't let anyone sway you from the sensible decision you made regarding the well-being of *your* child.

Hindsight is always 20/20. Many times at emotional downpoints in our lives, we are easily deceived by "Prince Harmings" disguised as "Prince Charmings."

However, we live, we learn and we move on. You courageously faced and championed your responsibility, while the "dysfunctional prince" chose leaving you to cope all by yourself. Now that you've done well and created a loving and [stable] home for your child, complete with a real "daddy," he wants to invade your happy home.

You have every right to label him as the "summer fling," for he truly does not deserve the title of "father." In this case, he's simply the *sperm donor*. He gave up all rights for fatherhood the moment he admonished that you "abort your baby." And he reinforced his decision by telling you to "leave him alone and get on with your life."

I agree with you for protecting your child from this individual because anyone who is simultaneously married to one woman [and] living with another, with two others pregnant, is definitely an unstable character.

Basic psychology and common sense relate that people don't readily change. They may alter their behavior to meet certain conditions, if it suits them, but eventually their true natures will resurface. For anyone to effectively change, they have to be reeducated and reprogrammed to move from one stage to another—otherwise the seemingly new behavior is only a temporary measure.

In response to the opinion that a child should know its natural parent, there's some gray area there. While I agree that the child should know *of* [its] natural parents, it's not necessary, nor advisable, for them to meet birth parents if the parents will bring chaos into the lives of innocent children.

When *you* feel your child is mature enough not to be influenced by an unstable personality, then gently and honestly share your truth with your child. You may also want to add that he/she has been blessed with a loving "daddy" who *chose* to adopt him/her because he/she is so very special and well-loved.

I think this sister is a winner for turning a situation that could have easily messed up her life into a winning environment for her baby. You go, sis!

"Mommy's Baby; Daddy's Maybe"

There's no similarity between *plotting* to have a baby and *planning* to have one. "Plotting" is trying to trap a man into marriage by purposely getting pregnant without his consent. Even though the brother should have used a condom, it is the sister who must take responsibility for her body. It's easy for an irresponsible man to run away from an unplanned pregnancy, but it is the sister who carries the pregnancy, so where is she going to run to? You've got to think before you act.

Now, this brings us to properly *planning* a pregnancy. "Planning" is having a child because you know you can give the child love, security, and a healthy environment to be nurtured in. There is a growing trend of single, successful, and financially secure sisters who are properly planning and giving birth to babies out of wedlock.

A LOVING HOME IS THE GREATEST GIFT YOU CAN GIVE A CHILD

Although I believe it is ideal to have a two-parent home for a child, I strongly believe that a single-parent home with lots of love is also a healthy environment for a child. There are also many single parents who adopt and do an excellent job of raising their children. The most important gifts you can give a child are love, a good education, and a strong sense of self.

PLANNING IS CONSTRUCTIVE; PLOTTING IS DESTRUCTIVE

Remember: Babies are a lifelong commitment. Make sure you are prepared to go the distance before you bring an innocent child into this world.

bad choice

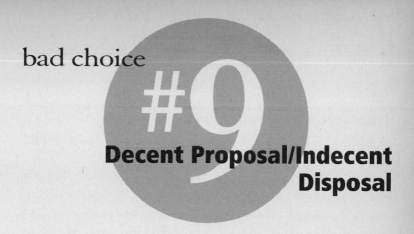

Decent Proposal/Indecent Disposal

Why is it that we always seem to gravitate toward the things that give us the most problems in life? Have you noticed the pattern in all the stories we have shared so far? The more the guy belittles and cheats, the harder the sister works to keep him.

One of the major reasons sisters are having such a difficult time connecting with ideal love is because all too often we bypass loving and nurturing men—labeling them as weaklings and wimps—for the pretentious, smooth-talking, good-for-nothing lover boys who end up being not exclusive lovers but *community lovers*—sharing themselves with at least two or three other sisters in the community.

Many sisters would rather live life on the edge, with a challenging and unpredictable playboy, than build a life with a stable and dependable man.

Twenty-eight-year-old Pamela confessed, "I don't want a 'honey-do' man. The kind that jumps every time I say 'honey, do this,' or 'honey, do that.' He would get on my nerves and bore me to death. I want a man who can light my fire and keep me guessing."

IF YOU'RE LOOKING FOR A MAN JUST TO FIRE YOUR TORCH, THEN DON'T COMPLAIN IF YOU END UP GETTING SCORCHED

Tragically, when a sister trades in a good man who is willing to love her for a bad one who is only willing to use her, she always ends up feeling sorry, but it's often too late.

Thirty-seven-year-old Myrna tearfully reported that she wished she could undo the damage she had caused in her life and her ex-husband's. She, a light-skinned sister with cover-girl looks, is a flight attendant. Jeffery, a dark-skinned, thirty-five-year-old brother with a stable outlook, is a civil-service worker. They met at a Labor Day barbecue at her brother's home a little over seven years ago. She had an eleven-year-old son from a previous marriage; he had never been married and had no children.

Jeffery was immediately attracted to Myrna. She said that she didn't initially find him attractive, but he pursued her relentlessly and she decided to date him. However, she was already involved with Scott, a married, German, self-employed businessman. She had been having an affair with Scott for three years. She was in love with Scott, but he had made it quite clear that he would never leave his wife. She started dating Jeffery. He treated her like a princess and did everything for her. She said she wanted to provide a two-parent household for her son, and since Scott would never marry her, and Jeffery was always there for her, she accepted his marriage proposal nine months after they had started dating.

CHOOSING A MAN ON THE REBOUND WILL EVENTUALLY TURN THINGS UPSIDE-DOWN

Jeffery paid all the bills. He would buy her anything his salary could afford. He would clean the house, cook the meals, do the laundry, run her baths, and give her foot massages. She said that he had her on a pedestal, and she "didn't have to lift a finger" to do a thing at home. She was never in love with Jeffery. It was a marriage of convenience. She still continued sleeping with Scott. It was easy for her to fool Jeffery because as a flight attendant, she was often away from home. Jeffery had no idea she was being unfaithful to him. When she was angry at Scott's refusal to dedicate himself to her completely, she would take out her rage on Jeffery. She would respond coldly to his touch, and she often pretended it was Scott who was in bed with her during their lovemaking. Ironically, the worse she treated Jeffery, the more he wanted to hold on to her.

Jeffery wanted Myrna to have their child. She took every precaution to ensure that this wouldn't happen. However, during a two-week getaway with Scott, she became pregnant. When she told Scott, he told her that he had warned her in the past not to get pregnant and that he didn't want to have anything to do with her anymore. He also warned her to abort the pregnancy, and said that if she didn't he would disown the child. She knew that because Scott was white and Jeffery was dark-skinned, she would not be able to pass off the baby as Jeffery's—so in agony, she had the abortion. She was angry and hurt because she really wanted to have Scott's baby. And every time Jeffery mentioned that he wanted to start a family with her, Myrna grew to resent him more.

Scott stopped seeing her. Jeffery had no clue about the affair. Myrna just didn't care anymore. For a year, she had a series of one-night stands in the various places her job took her.

Too Many Lies Destroy Too Many Lives

The following year, Myrna did get pregnant by Jeffery. But she had no intention of having a child with him, so she aborted it. Jeffery found out by accident from the medical receipts. He didn't want to believe it, and he asked her about it. She told him it was true. He was broken and asked her why. She didn't hold back, tearfully blurting out, "I got rid of it because I didn't want a black baby like you." As he stood there dumbfounded and in tears, she kept screaming and wailing, "I hate to look at you. I hate you. Because of you, I couldn't keep my other baby. Why don't you just leave me! Get out!" She told him the whole story about Scott and the previous abortion. Jeffery was a broken man. He left.

Myrna's story doesn't end here. She said that she felt an emptiness when Jeffery left. She realized she had no one, and she didn't want to end up being by herself. She told me that after six weeks Jeffery called and told her he still wanted to be with her. And he was willing to forgive her, as long as she promised not to cheat again. She apologized and they got back together. The first few months were awkward, but soon after, Jeffery fell back into the routine of catering to Myrna. And Myrna kept using birth-control pills without his knowing it. After about ten months, her feelings of resentment toward him started to surface again.

INDECENT DISPOSAL, DISPOSES INDECENTLY

Myrna cheated on Jeffery again. This time it was with their next-door neighbor, a forty-three-year-old Irish man named Richard. Everyone in the neighborhood soon became privy to the gossip— everyone but Jeffery. The affair carried on for four months, until one day Jeffery came home in the middle of the afternoon and found Myrna feeding Richard lunch in their bed. Both were naked.

Myrna reported that he just stood there, looked at her with tears in his eyes, shook his head in disappointment, and pleaded, "Baby, how could you? This is the lowest of the low. This one I can never forgive you for." He looked defeated and he left.

He meant it. When I first met Myrna, two years had passed since his departure from the marriage.

IF YOU BEAT A BROTHER TO THE GROUND, DON'T YOU CRY WHEN HE WON'T STICK AROUND

I met Myrna at a Thanksgiving dinner at the home of my sister, Angie, who is an interior decorator. Myrna had been one of Angie's decorating clients in the past, and they had become good friends. Angie, who has a generous and kind heart, knew her story and didn't want Myrna to spend the holidays alone. Myrna volunteered to give the Thanksgiving blessings, and she broke down hysterically during her prayer. I asked what was wrong, and Angie came over to me and whispered that Myrna was going through a hard time and asked me if I could try to help her. I took her into the living room; we sat and she opened up to me. She said that the only time Jeffery had ever spoken to her after the breakup was to ask for a divorce. He had come and gotten his clothes, and was living within a ten-mile radius of his former home. She had seen him a few times when she'd gone out, and he had ignored her and driven right past her. She had telephoned him numerous times, and he had hung up on her. She openly confessed that she wanted him back.

MYRNA: I know I was wrong. I am so sorry now. I want him back, but he won't even talk to me. I am not going to give him a divorce. *(Crying)* I want my husband back.

DR. CORNISH: Have you thought about why you want him now?

MYRNA: Because I love him. I want him back.

DR. CORNISH: Why did you do those awful things to him?

MYRNA: I wanted him to be strong. I just wanted him to tell me to stop. He let me walk all over him and he never stopped me. I had no respect for him.

DR. CORNISH: Because he was kind to you?

MYRNA: No, because he was so weak. He was too easy. He had me on a pedestal and I took him for granted.

DR. CORNISH: Why did you?

MYRNA: Because I didn't think he was good enough for me. *(Crying hysterically)* All my life I've been told that anything too black is never too good . . . and I didn't want a dark-skinned baby. I wanted Scott's baby.

DR. CORNISH: Jesus! *(Pause)* Then why did you lead the man on and marry him? *(Pause)* Myrna, are you hurt because you think you love him now and miss him, or are you really upset because *he* left *you*?

MYRNA: *(Pause)* Both . . . I'm so sorry for what I did. He was so kind to me. I love him now. And he left me. He was so good to me.

DR. CORNISH: He was. And you took advantage of him. You had a decent man who loved you. Whatever his reasons may have been, he loved you anyway. And that's all that should have mattered. But you walked all over him. He even forgave you when he found out you cheated the first time. But to add insult to injury, you did it again; and with his neighbor; and in your matrimonial bed. Come on, now, that's really pretty bad. I don't mean to upset you even further, but if he comes back to you, he has no respect for himself. After the way you treated him, you have to be realistic with yourself and realize that after all this time, he probably isn't coming back.

MYRNA: I don't want to hear that. No, no, no . . .

DR. CORNISH: Myrna, get a grip on yourself. Stop doing this to yourself. Stop putting your life on hold and punishing yourself like this. You've made a terrible mistake. But learn from it and move on now. All you can do is apologize to him. Let it go. Forgive yourself and move on . . . just don't ever take someone's kindness for granted again.

IF YOU'VE MADE A MISTAKE, ADMIT IT, APOLOGIZE, AND MOVE ON

We continued this conversation for the remainder of the evening. But Myrna wasn't ready to move on. She refused to accept that Jeffery had been hurt so badly by her that he wasn't coming back. Myrna has truly messed up her life and is now taking antidepressant drugs to help her deal with her severe mood swings. But she still refuses to let go of Jeffery and seek counseling to move on.

CONDITIONING FROM THE PAST CAN BE YOUR WORST ENEMY

The saddest part about Myrna's saga is that she threw away a relationship with a decent black man because of the damaging conditioning she received from her upbringing. She treated him badly because he was the wrong shade for her. Poor Myrna is just a product of her environment. As sisters, we each have our individual issues—for some it's skin coloring, for others it's weight, and still others face low, or no, self-worth because of the dysfunctions they grew up with. If we don't seek to correct our individual issues, we will always hurt either ourselves or others all the way through life.

TAKE A CRITICAL LOOK BACKWARD SO YOU CAN MAKE A CRUCIAL MOVE FORWARD

Let me share my own story with you here. I would be a hypocrite if I didn't include myself in this chapter. I humbly admit that I've also hurt some really decent black men in the past. Let me use myself as an example to demonstrate how you have to get to the root of the problem in order to correct it.

The turning point in my life came at the age of twenty-four. I had met Shaun at a birthday party the previous year at my aunt's home. He was a very handsome and kind twenty-six-year-old biracial black man. I had left a previous relationship less than two weeks before, and I was not looking to get into another right away. He approached me, started a conversation, and stood by my side all evening. We found each other fascinating. We exchanged interesting stories about our lives and the career directions we were pursuing. He shared that he was managing his family's business, a popular and upscale health-food restaurant, and that he also owned a lucrative vending-machine business. I shared that I had a substantial position as a retail executive in the World Trade Center and that I had taken a few years off since graduating from college to learn about living and working in the "real world" before going to graduate school.

He asked me out. We exchanged numbers. I told him up front that I wasn't looking for a serious relationship, but we started dating. He treated me like a little queen. He wined and dined me, bought all sorts of presents and surprises—but even though I was dating him exclusively, my heart wasn't into it. The more stoic I was toward him, the more he seemed to pursue me. On several occasions when he pleaded with me as to why I was so nonchalant toward our relationship, I simply answered, "I don't want to lead you on. If you don't like it, then start seeing other people." During that summer, after we had been involved for seven months, he told me that he had fallen in love with me, and he gave me five thousand dollars and a diamond necklace as a present for my twenty-fourth birthday. I never lied to him. I had to be honest with him—I told him that I wasn't in love with him, but that I liked him very much. Everyone would tell me how lucky I was to have such a rich, handsome, and generous guy in love with me. But I would just shrug it off and coldly and sarcastically remark, "Big deal. He's the one who is lucky to have me."

IF YOU DON'T ERASE THE COLD, YOU CAN NEVER EMBRACE THE GOLD

He would call me practically every night, and many times I was at home, but let my answering machine pick up the phone anyway. I felt that he was crowding my space too much, and I got annoyed when he wanted to see me too often. During the Christmas holidays he invited me to his parents' home for dinner, and I refused because I didn't want to get too close to him. That really hurt him.

He stormed away and said, "That's it. I can't take this anymore. Nothing I do seems to please you." For a split second, I almost cried, but I caught myself and occupied my mind with other holiday plans with family and friends at work.

Before New Year's Eve he was back with an apology and a plea that we try to make it work. I let him back into my life physically, but emotionally, I continued to be unavailable to him. His birthday was the day before Valentine's Day. About a month before his birthday, he asked me if I would attend a special celebration for both occasions at his family's home. The word "family" scared me—it was too serious for me—so I refused. This was the breaking point for him. He lashed out, "What kind of girlfriend are you? It seems that I only get to see you two or three times a month." And again, believe it or not, I casually responded, "If you are not happy, then go see someone else."

"Is that what you want?" He asked. "Yes," I responded. "Stop pressuring me into a serious relationship." I still can remember the sadness in his eyes as he left. That time I really began to feel bad for my actions. I didn't hear from him for the next three weeks, and I started thinking about how horrible I had been to him. I didn't question why I had done it; I just moved to the next phase and promised myself I would start to treat him better.

IF YOU'VE CONSTANTLY CHASED HIM AWAY, THEN DON'T GET UPSET WHEN HE HAS GONE ASTRAY

I decided to surprise him and go to his Valentine's/birthday party. My sister, Angie, and one of her girlfriends went with me. When we got there, he hadn't arrived yet. After about twenty minutes, he arrived accompanied by a woman. When he saw me he was shocked. He came over and said, "I didn't expect to see you. You told me to leave you alone."

"Are you seeing someone else?" I wanted to know. He held his head down and wouldn't look me in the eyes. "How dare you cheat on me?"

"I'd given you my heart and you turned me away," he confessed. "What did you expect me to do?"

"How could you?" I admonished, "I'll never forgive you for this. I don't ever want to see you again." As he stood there in tears, asking me to understand, I wouldn't listen. I was more concerned with my being put in a compromising situation than with the pain this brother was expressing to me. I walked out and left him standing there.

He called several times after and asked if I would forgive him and resume the relationship. I refused him.

The nerve of me, huh? What a drama queen I was. It was all a subconscious act—an act I wasn't even aware I was performing. It was a cover-up to protect myself from the emotions that go along with the territory of being in love. I didn't want to ever again experience the pain I had felt when I had broken my engagement to Daniel, my college boyfriend and first love, three and a half years before. But at that moment with Shaun, I was feeling the same pain I had been running away from. So I was at a major turning point in my life. I had to make a decision fast: "Do I continue to bury my emotions and pretend that I'm above feeling emotional pain, or do I face the pain and find out why I've been running away from my emotions?"

YOU'VE GOT TO LOOK INTERNALLY IN ORDER TO CORRECT PROBLEMS EXTERNALLY

Fortunately, I chose the more difficult, yet healthier path: I decided I had to face myself and peel away the layers of protective coating I had subconsciously adopted to protect my center. My God, it was hard. Sis, it's the hardest thing to face yourself, flaws and all, and be completely vulnerable and candid about the experiences and events in your life that have formed the person you are in the present. You have to work backward from where you are right now, and go through the series of occurrences.

To find out why I had treated this decent man so unkindly, I went back to the relationship before this one. I looked into it, and my behavior had been the same. In that relationship I ran away immediately after Colin got down on one knee in my living room and asked for my hand in marriage. He was a nice, handsome, and brilliant young and upcoming securities broker on Wall Street. We had dated for a year. He had gotten too close. I was scared and ran away, hurting him horribly. This was a pattern for me. I had to review my first relationship, where my concept of love had initially been formed. Same thing there—I met Daniel at seventeen, during my second semester in college. It was love at first sight for the both of us. Six months after we started dating, I lost my virginity to him; one month later we were engaged. One of the reasons why we got engaged so soon was because I had grown up with a father who had adamantly preached that pre-marital sex is a sin (this rule applied to his daughters only—to my brothers he taught the complete opposite). I felt guilty because of this, and I ran into the engagement, and then after two years of being engaged, I honestly felt trapped. I knew I wanted to travel and see the world before getting married.

Daniel put me through a guilt trip when I told him that we had rushed in too soon. He was hurting and refused to let go. It took me over one year, many sleepless nights, and a lot of tears to gather enough strength to give myself permission to leave the engagement. Now I can understand his reasoning, but I shouldered that guilt and carried it with me into the other relationships.

My guilt led to unconscious self-sabotage. I had experienced such a long and painful breakup with Daniel that I didn't want to cause anyone else that hurt, and I didn't want to experience that pain again. So I figured that if I stayed away from falling in love, and kept my emotions out of relationships, no one would get hurt. But in trying to deny myself, I was actually unintentionally hurting others in the process. In every situation, I would always say up front, "If you ever want to leave, let me know, and I won't try to keep you, because I know what it's like trying to get out when some one wants to hold on."

DISSOLVE YOUR OLD SCAR AND BECOME A NEW STAR

Seeing my mother killed in front of me as a child, and then growing up in a dysfunctional household headed by my dad, who yelled and spanked more often than he reasoned, I was conditioned to believe two things: Don't love anyone too much or they will leave you, and don't be too vulnerable or you'll be punished for it. So at sixteen, I graduated from high school and literally ran away to an out-of-state college. And for that period in time Daniel became my new family. That's why the guilt was so heavy—because I felt I had betrayed and abandoned him after he was there for me through those important years.

This is why in my therapy sessions, I guide clients into healing the wounded child within. Your early upbringing is the foundation upon which your personality and actions are built. Everyone comes from some sort of dysfunctional background. It's a reality and is nothing to be ashamed of. The *Leave It to Beaver* and *Father Knows Best* family shows are just that—shows. They are ideal dreams, but are not a reality for 80 percent of the American population—and even less a reality for 95 percent of the African-American population. In actuality, you are not responsible for where you came from. But you are responsible for where you are now, and for where you are going from here.

GET RID OF THE PAST SO YOU CAN BE FREE AT LAST

This turning point in my life was well over ten years ago, and I can honestly say that I've never disrespected a decent black man since. Had I not analyzed myself and broken the cycle, I would be repeating the same mistakes today. Like you, I have "been there, done that." The beauty about life is that wherever you are, you can stop and heal the moment you choose to do so. But you must be honest with yourself. Part of my internal work was that I had to make peace with my dad. And today, he is one of the greatest joys in my life. I was lucky enough to be able to contact the three decent men I've hurt in the past and sincerely apologize for my inability to love them at the time. But I explained that I had done the best I could with what I had known at that young age. All three were really supportive and forgiving. And we are on good speaking terms today.

It took a lot of courage for me to open myself up like this with you, but I believe we learn by real-life examples. And as an example, I have to practice what I preach. The advice I share here is not the result of theories or controlled classroom studies. These are real-life experiences of sisters like you and me.

From my own personal experience, and from the experiences of the countless other women I've advised, believe me when I tell you that the first place to start is to stop the "get them before they get you" attitude. Brothers hurt too. Black men do cry. Taking a man for granted is unfair. Break the cycle.

IF YOU KEEP LOOKING FOR A MAN TO COMPLETE YOU, INSTEAD OF ONE TO COMPLEMENT YOU, SOMETHING IS WRONG

When sisters are asked what we are looking for in a mate, most will share, "I want a man who is decent, kind, honest, sensitive, and not afraid to show emotions." But when we get such a man, we don't appreciate him—we take him for granted, still in search of a more "challenging" man.

I'm sure there's a different reason for each sister's personal preference—one person might be influenced by the particular time in her life and another by her age, and still another could be looking for the bad-boy image from the big screen. Whatever the deep-seated reason is, to have a fulfilling relationship with a decent man each of us must look deep within to find out what our individual motives are, or else we'll keep searching for completion in others. And when we don't find it in them—which we never will—we will drop them and keep searching. Your own completion can only come from within you.

Quite often we bypass the good guys and choose the challenging (i.e., turbulent) relationships because it always gives us something to occupy ourselves with. It makes us avoid looking at our own flaws. For example, if you keep yourself busy trying to correct someone else's behavior, or nursing the heartache he is causing you, you are too busy to look at what may really be wrong in your life. Twenty-six-year-old Rachon shared, "I always get involved with the hard-to-get guys because they keep me on my toes. Even though it hurts sometimes, I'm always wondering what they'll do next. This way I don't have to face how screwed up my life is."

YES—BLACK MEN DO CRY!

Here's a letter I received from one of my male readers of the *New York Beacon:*

> Dear Dr. Cornish:
>
> I am a 41-year-old Black male photo-journalist. I am very sensitive and caring and the women I have been involved with have often mistaken this for weakness. I got married as soon as I finished college at the age of 21. I found out eight years into the marriage that my wife had been having a three-year relationship with my best friend. We had two children and, in spite of her infidelity, I wanted to keep our family together. But, she wanted out, so we divorced.
>
> In my early thirties, I remarried. I helped to put my second wife through medical school and as soon as she became an M.D., she fell in love with another man. I was in love

with her and I tried to keep the relationship together, but she refused.

Now I'm in my early forties and I am afraid of commitment and afraid to trust. Black women claim they want a caring Black man, but when you give your all, they seem to walk all over you. Now, my second wife wants to get back into my life, but I have no love or respect left for her.

I haven't given up on Black women and I do want to get married, but how can I learn to trust again?

J. W., New York, NY

Dear J. W.:

You should be commended for being such a sensitive and compassionate man in spite of what you've been through. It is unfortunate, but true, that many men and women often mistake kindness for weakness.

Good for you that you have gained enough self-respect and dignity to move on from an estranged and disrespectful mate. I'm pleased to know that you do not judge all Black women by the incompatible marriages you've had. It takes a strong man to be so truthful and forgiving.

To learn to trust again, you must first believe in your self-worth. From your letter, it seems that you've given more love than you've gotten. You must screen all potential mates before entering into another relationship. Sum each one up by these three very important questions:

1. Does her presence enrich my life in any way?
2. Is she looking out for my best interest?
3. Does she like me for the individual I am?

If you can answer "yes" to all three, then there is an excellent chance that you've finally found the right mate for you. If you answer "no" to any, then keep looking.

My advice to you is not to change yourself, but to change

your choice. There are many single, loving and caring Black women from whom you can choose wisely—one who is willing to blend her mind, body and spirit with yours—that you may both enjoy the beautiful totality of unconditional love.

KNOW WHEN TO BE BOLD AND WHEN TO PUT THE OPINIONS OF OTHERS ON HOLD

"Girl, dump him. You don't need him. What an idiot. A damn thirty-six-year-old black man, and he still can't get his act together. He's going to wait until he's fifty friggin' years old before he wakes up and realizes it's too damn late to grow up. They are all the same. Bastards . . ." Trica's voice echoed on the other end of the line as Janet listened intently.

Janet, a black thirty-four-year-old fashion editor, and Keith, a black insurance salesman, had been dating for seven months. The relationship had begun intensely, but Keith decided it was moving a little too fast and wanted to slow things down a bit. Janet called her best girlfriend Trica for support. Within this seven-month period, Trica, single and uninvolved, had been thoroughly briefed on all information concerning Keith—from his name, date of birth, and address, to his occupation, hobbies, and sexual habits. She, in turn, found it her duty to share this information with two other girlfriends, Stacey and Valarie, both also single and uninvolved.

Within hours of the breakup, Janet's phone rang. The girl-friends were calling to give support. Janet was appreciative when they first arrived to keep her company. But was this conversation doing her any good? The chorus chanted, "Girl, I told you not to trust any man completely." "I swear, black men think they are God's gift to women." "That's why I'm staying celibate. I have no time for these silly games."

Janet's sister-friends meant well. Unfortunately, the conversation had more to do with their pain and disappointment with black men in general than it had to do with Janet and Keith's individual situation. Luckily for Janet, she did not let her friends influence her decision to be with Keith. After two weeks had passed, she called him. She had come to realize that he had had no intention of hurting her; he had gotten cold feet. She loved him with patience and caution, and they have been married for three years now.

Had Janet bought into the misconceptions of the sisterhood, she too would still be wondering, "Why are all the good black men gone?"

LET'S LOSE THE RAGE AND FIND THE REMEDY

There is a major communication gap between black men and women. Bashing black men will not help the plight of black women. When we belittle black men, we belittle a part of ourselves.

The sisterhood among black women is a cushion we all need. However, there is a point at which it becomes toxic, when sisters get together and chorus about how awful black relationships are.

It's good to have a support circle of sisters to help us get through life's rough spots (and there are many), but to dwell in the circle, not knowing where to draw the line, is defeating. Interference from girlfriends can be damaging when it focuses on the negative instead of the positive. Sisters can meet each other in a department store, a rest room, or on a bus, exchange phone numbers, and right away start talking about the problem with a man, or the problem with not having a man, or the problem with so-and-so's man.

If you believe that black men are unworthy, then you are subconsciously placing a barrier between yourself and any potential connection with a black man. How can you expect to have a healthy relationship if you have already perceived it to be unhealthy? There is a vast gulf between black men and black women. Since healthy black relationships are the cornerstones of healthy black families, this gulf affects all of our futures.

INCREASE THE PEACE BETWEEN THE MISTERS AND THE SISTERS

Black women and men are at odds in relationships. We each claim we don't know what the other wants. We all play these unnecessary games, so that no one knows what's actually real or what's fake anymore. Black relationships seem to have gotten caught in the undercurrent of society's backlash and drifted out to sea.

At this point it doesn't even matter where it started. The point is, where is it going? We have got to break the black-on-black bashing cycle.

It is frightening how quickly we conform to the derogatory popular belief that "all black men are dogs" when we have disagreements with brothers. As we can see from Janet's example in the above story, all relationships take patience and understanding. All cultures have relationship problems, but have you ever heard it openly declared that "all *white* men are dogs," "all *Asian* men are dogs," "all *Jewish* men are dogs," or "all *Indian* men are dogs"?

Black relationships are constantly being viewed under the critical microscope of society at large. Over two decades ago the mainstream media created the myth of the "good black men" shortage. Unfortunately, too many sisters and brothers have bought into that myth.

Dr. Gwendolyn Goldsby-Grant, in her best-selling book *The Best Kind of Loving: A Black Woman's Guide to Finding Intimacy,* shares, "Relationship issues among black women and men are . . . more complex than those of white women and men. Although there are certainly tremendous overlaps in many of the fundamental issues that we all struggle with, such as self-esteem, loneliness, fear, control and power, there are also profound differences. In addition to the social dynamics that affect male-female communications in general, as African-Americans, we carry the added burden of the myths and stereotypes that grow out of our real history of slavery, second-class citizenship and economic disenfranchisement."

We have to be sensitive to the complex nature of our relationships and learn to be realistic in our expectations for black men.

SIS, GET REAL; CHOOSE A MAN WHO CARES HOW YOU FEEL!

A truly balanced life is made up of four components: God, health, money, and love. Black women are clever, witty, and smart. We have grown to be so self-sufficient that we can manage the first three components on our own, yet we keep falling short in the love department.

Why is it that we are so quick to dump the decent black men, but chase after the reckless users? This reminds me of the biblical proverb that says "If a man has one hundred sheep, and one of them should go astray, doesn't he leave the ninety-nine and go into the mountains looking for the estranged one? And if he finds it, I tell you, he is happier about that one sheep than the ninety-nine that didn't go astray."

Maybe it is human nature to go after the more difficult things in life—but when the difficulty causes too much pain, I say it's time to use your God-given gift of *free will* and choose a loyal man, form a team, and face life's difficulties together.

TWO WRONGS DON'T MAKE IT RIGHT

Many sisters who have been hurt in previous relationships have made vows to themselves that they will never give their hearts fully to any man again. They have adopted the "Do unto others before they do unto you" survival code. And all too often the nice guy gets entangled in the web of the sister's pain. Thirty-four-year-old Crystal admits, "I was hurt badly in the past by my first love. This guy was my world. He meant everything to me. I trusted him with my life. And after being with him for eight years, I caught him with my own cousin. I thought I was going to die. I learned never to ever trust a man again. I've met a few guys who told me they love me and all that, but I don't care who it is, I get rid of them before I grow too close to them. And if they hurt, hey, if I can get over it, so can they."

Get Rid of the "Struck and Stuck in the Pain of the Past" Syndrome

If someone has caused you hurt, then confront that person and get it out of your system—number one, for your own well-being, and number two, for the well-being of a potential decent mate. Look at it this way: Why should you deny yourself happiness with a caring love, just because someone else has hurt you in the past? That person who has done the hurt has already moved on and is not thinking about you, so why are you keeping yourself in yesterday's misery? Today is a new beginning.

Sis, empty your baggage of past hurts—as a matter of fact, let's throw away all the past baggage, and get a brand-new set of luggage. Make a promise to yourself to take a new trip in life. Get off the old beaten path of unhealthy love, and allow yourself to journey on a new road, side by side with a willing and deserving decent man.

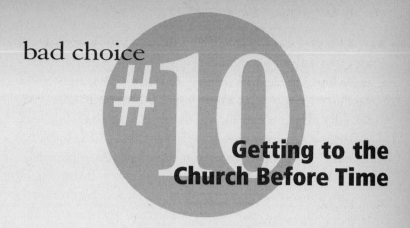

bad choice

#10

Getting to the Church Before Time

The French have a clever epigram on the subject of marriage: "Marriage is like a besieged fortress: Those who are outside want to get in; those who are inside want to get out."

Although this observation may seem a bit cynical, there is a lot of truth in it. Many sisters have suffered a lot of psychological and emotional misery in their marriages. But the reason they have suffered is because all too often they have prematurely rushed into marriages with incompatible mates. The marriage itself is not the problem—the problem is the unrealistic expectations we take into marriages.

GIVING TOO MUCH, TOO SOON, MAKES YOU AN EASY TARGET

One of the saddest cases I've ever seen of rushing into marriage too soon is thirty-four-year-old Myrtle. She had experienced a series of bad relationships in her twenties and decided to take a break from seeing anyone for a while. Myrtle had been celibate for six years before she met thirty-seven-year-old Glen. She worked as a receptionist, and he worked as a delivery man who made frequent deliveries to her office building. They met and started a conversation while waiting for the elevator in the lobby of her building one morning.

He invited her to dinner that evening, and she accepted. They met after work. He bought flowers for her, and they dined at a nearby restaurant. During dinner, Glen took an intense interest in Myrtle's background. Myrtle enjoyed the attention and answered all of Glen's inquiries—including information about her social, professional, and financial backgrounds. One of the things she found a bit strange was his keen interest in her credit status. When she assured him that her credit was "squeaky-clean," he remarked, "You're the type of responsible woman I need in my life. I will take such good care of you. I want to be your protector and provider in a relationship." Instead of questioning his motive for such a personal declaration on a first date, she was flattered by his compliment.

She neglected to ask about his background. However, he volunteered that he had been divorced for two years and had two daughters with his previous wife of nine years.

If in Doubt, You've Got to Check Him Out!

After their first date, Myrtle and Glen started seeing each other as a couple. Glen called her at least four times each day and picked her up from work every evening. She was especially attracted to him because he bought flowers for her every week. After six weeks of dating, he proposed. She was elated, but was apprehensive at the same time. She felt a bit uneasy when he kept pressing her to set a wedding date for three months following his proposal. But, with further flattery from him, she obliged.

Two weeks after she accepted his proposal, Glen told Myrtle that he needed her social security number. He said he also needed access to her credit cards because he wanted to add her to his bank account. Although she had a strong hunch advising her against this, she was flattered that he "trusted her enough to add her to his savings account." So, she surrendered to his demands.

A few weeks later, he told her he wanted to buy a home for

her. He said that he couldn't afford it on his salary alone, and he needed her to "work with him" toward this goal. He convinced her to "trust him" with her personal savings of sixteen thousand dollars, to be used as a down payment on their future home. Again, she obliged. By the time Myrtle attended my workshop, Glen had already convinced her to also contribute her weekly earnings into his care for their future goals.

In the workshop, Myrtle freely admitted that she had uneasy feelings about marrying Glen, but she confessed that she was tired of being single and living by herself.

DR. CORNISH: From the information you shared, he doesn't seem legitimate at all. Do you know anything about his background?

MYRTLE: I know where he works and where he lives.

DR. CORNISH: Is that all? And this is the man you're planning to marry? You've given this man all of your vital information, and you don't know anything else about him? Do you know his social security number?

MYRTLE: No.

DR. CORNISH: But you gave him yours? Oh, boy—something isn't right here. You need to find out more. I think you should have this man checked out thoroughly before you get married to him.

MYRTLE: I'm not sure if he has lied to me.

DR. CORNISH: Sis, for your sake I hope not. But there's only one way of being sure. You obviously don't trust him, or else you wouldn't be harboring these doubts. Pay attention to your intuition. It doesn't cost to get a background check— just search the public records, and go through the Department of Motor Vehicles.

MYRTLE: I don't know. I'll just see what happens.

DR. CORNISH: From your expression, I think you are afraid of what you'll find out about this man. I know you've been alone for a while, and you really want to make this work. But being lonely is no excuse for running into a marriage that could end up causing you more harm than happiness. If you're so doubtful about him, either leave him or check him out. But you've got to do something.

USING A GUPPY TO CATCH A WHALE

I was worried about Myrtle leaving herself so vulnerable. About five months later, I received a desperate phone call from her. Myrtle confessed that she had avoided looking into Glen's background when I had advised her to, because she didn't want to discover anything that would have "spoiled" her marriage plans. So she had ignored her reservations and married him. He ended up using her money and credit status to purchase a house that was in foreclosure. He had an affair with the tenant who occupied the ground-floor apartment of their home.

When Myrtle confronted him about the affair, he became hostile and physically abusive. That was when she decided to do a security check on him. She was flooded with disturbing information about Glen. She found out that he was still legally married to his second wife. He had been in jail several times—once for molesting a seven-year-old child. He was currently out on probation. And he had to meet with a probation officer every Wednesday.

She discovered that when she had met him, all he had had in savings was $1,200. This is what I call "using a guppy to catch a whale." He had preyed upon her gullibility. He had used his small savings (the guppy) to lure her in with the promise of making her his beneficiary. Instead of looking into the facts, she had gotten hooked, and had ended up losing her larger savings (the whale) to him. She left him and threatened to sue if he didn't return her money.

GIRL, PULL YOURSELF TOGETHER!

But here's what I found most astonishing of all: She hadn't called me because she needed help coping with her mistake. She had called because she was upset that he hadn't called her or tried to get her back.

DR. CORNISH: Are you serious? This guy is a nasty stain on the fabric of society, and you're sitting at home pining over him—you've got to be joking!

MYRTLE: It's not that. He hasn't even called to say sorry or anything.

DR. CORNISH: Sorry? You need to have his sorry behind thrown in jail for bigamy. Myrtle, don't tell me you would consider taking this guy back if he apologized?

MYRTLE: I don't know. I really don't know.

"LEARNING TO LOVE YOURSELF IS THE GREATEST LOVE OF ALL"

DR. CORNISH: Myrtle, you need to take your focus off this child molester and focus on why you think so little of yourself. You're very wounded and hurt right now. The only way you're going to heal and recover from this is if you concentrate on becoming the best *you* that you can be. Don't you think you deserve to find true happiness?

MYRTLE: Ummm . . . yeah.

DR. CORNISH: Don't you think after all of this mess, you deserve peace of mind?

MYRTLE: Yeah.

DR. CORNISH: Do you think it's sensible to have this no-class, low-life crook around you?

MYRTLE: No.

DR. CORNISH: Good! Let's concentrate on healing you so you can move on.

KICK THE SOCIAL PRESSURES TO THE CURB

I cannot emphasize this enough: *Don't ever get married just for the sake of being married.* Women don't *need* to get married today. Get married because you've found a loving companion and you *want* to spend your life with him.

The *Sleeping Beauty* fairy tale is a ridiculous role model for sisters. It describes some helpless woman who spends her life in a deep slumber. And she can wake up to reality only when some fantasy prince comes along and rescues her with a magical kiss . . . and they "live happily ever after." Give me a break! Marriage is a beautiful bonding when you have two intelligent and mature people who come together out of mutual respect. Choose a friend first. Don't feel pressured because you want to prove to others that you are "marriage material," or because you feel your biological clock is ticking too rapidly.

THE SIX-MONTH HITCH; THE ONE-YEAR DITCH

At one time couples faced two major hurdles in marriage—"the seven-year itch" and the "twenty-year ditch." It was popular belief that after seven years of marriage, a man would get the urge, or an "itch," to have an outside affair, and that after twenty years of marriage, he would leave his wife for another, usually younger, woman, when he experienced a midlife crisis.

However, at the rapid rate at which couples now rush into marriage, without first getting to know the vital characteristics of intended lifelong partners, the cycle of the traditional seven-year itch and twenty-year ditch has been dramatically shortened. The modified version reflects what I call the "six-month hitch" and the "one-year ditch." Couples are taking the "revolving door" policy into their unions—they are walking in quickly and rotating out rapidly.

Debra, twenty-eight, had had a whirlwind two-month courtship with Kevin, twenty-nine, when he proposed to her. Four months after his proposal, they decided to "jump the broom" into matrimonial bliss together. He was the perfect gentleman and treated her with kindness and much affection. He was a young, successful film director, with a promising career in front of him. She was poised, well-spoken, and part-owner of a successful travel agency.

They had a beautiful, exquisite, and elaborate wedding. It included three hundred guests and ten bridesmaids escorted by ten groomsmen. Debra's best girlfriend, Tracey, served as her maid of honor. Kevin's fraternity brother and longtime friend, Gary, stood up as his best man.

They moved into a spacious suburban home, complete with the white picket fence and an adorable French poodle named Brittany.

Just three short months after their dream wedding, Debra noticed a distinct change in Kevin's behavior. The undivided attention he had once showered on her was now turned to his work, his out-of-town business trips, and his hanging out with the guys.

"LOVE DON'T LIVE HERE ANYMORE"

In the beginning, it had seemed as if Kevin couldn't get enough of Debra sexually. Now it seemed as if she had to beg him to have intercourse with her. She was puzzled by his drastic change. She had a sinking feeling in her stomach as she began to suspect he was having an affair. She continued to try to be supportive and lovable. But, as time elapsed, he became more distant and unreachable.

On several occasions, she tried to discuss the change in his behavior with him. He would simply answer, "You are over-reacting." After another month, he started getting verbally abusive and would become annoyed with her for no reason at all. He would often admonish, "We are just not compatible." When she probed further, he became hostile and shouted, "I don't owe you an explanation. I wish you would just leave my house. We are just not compatible." She always cried, but never left.

On their first anniversary, Debra prepared a special dinner for Kevin. He came home late, as usual. When she told him he could have been more a little more considerate because of the special day, he lost his temper. He punched her, spat in her face, and told her he hated her. She managed to get to a phone and call the police.

Kevin was arrested. Debra got a restraining order against him. But she still wanted to make the marriage work. When he got out of jail he refused to have anything to do with her, and he filed for divorce.

Kevin was not allowed near the house, so Debra packed his belongings to have them sent to his new address. While she went through his personal belongings, she came across a letter that confirmed the affair she had suspected he was having all along. But the contents revealed more than she had bargained for.

It was a love letter filled with references to the intimate times shared on frequent getaway rendezvous. She thought it couldn't get any worse, but the ending traumatized her ever further. It was signed, "Yours to love forever and always, Gary."

Kevin had been having a secret homosexual relationship with the "longtime friend" who had been his best man at his wedding.

DOUBLE DECEIT IS DOUBLY DEVASTATING

This secret practice of bisexual black men has devastated many un-suspecting sisters. It's bad enough to discover your spouse is mess-ing around. But the betrayal is twice as painful when his infidelity is with someone of the same sex.

Dr. Rosie Milligan, best-selling author of *Satisfying the Black Man Sexually,* shares, "Some may have bisexual tendencies all their lives. Some may never respond to those urges, but others may frequently slip in and out of their sexual preferences their whole lives."

"BROTHERS BEHAVING BADLY"

This is a taboo subject that many people don't like to discuss. But pretending it doesn't exist will not make it go away. The deceit is unfortunate, but it's also a reality. A reality that you should keep your eyes open for—to avoid being an innocent victim, like the sister in this letter I received from a reader of my advice column in the *New York Beacon*:

Dear Dr. Cornish:

I am a 24-year-old gay Black man. I'm an only child and my mother and I have a close and loving relationship. She has always taught me to be honest and to be proud of who I am. However, I neither act nor look the stereotypical way most people think of when the hear the term "gay." I am an aspiring model and women are always attracted to me and want me to ask them out. I've been a homosexual since I was 15 years old and I don't want to mislead a woman in any way. I have never had a relationship with a woman.

For the past eleven months I've been dating an attractive, macho-looking 39-year-old Black cop who is a closet bisexual. He lives with his straight girlfriend and they have been together for a little over three years.

He invited me to their home for his birthday party and introduced me to her as one of his buddies from work. His girlfriend is Black, 34 years old and a nurse, and she pays most of the bills in their home, while he buys me gifts and helps me pay my rent.

I have fallen in love with him, and I am hurt and upset over his dual lifestyle. I've confronted him about making a decision as to which one of us he really wants to be with and he keeps telling me not to pressure him or else he will have to let me go.

I am very angry at this and I believe he's using me and his unsuspecting girlfriend to selfishly enjoy the "best of both worlds."

I'm writing to ask you if I should tell her what he's really like.

T. L., Brooklyn, NY

LORD—SAVE A SISTER FROM THIS DECEITFUL MISTER

Dear T. L.:

It's amazing how people *conveniently* decide to be "honest" when it suits their individual needs. While you have been truthful about being homosexual, you were not honest when you entered into that woman's home pretending to be her man's working buddy—while in actuality, you are his sleeping buddy.

Honesty is not like an article of clothing you casually decide to put on or take off depending on the mood of the moment as displayed by your confused "macho-looking" Casanova's lifestyle. "Should I wear red or blue today, should I have a man or a woman tonight?"

How dare he jeopardize his unsuspecting mate's life and trust? She does have a right to know the truth, but not from you! What you call your truth is "dishonest." It is not coming from a concerned soul looking out for her well-being, but rather from a scorned heart seeking revenge.

You have every right to be hurt and upset by his duality. However, examine your true motive for wanting to tell his girlfriend. Ask yourself whether or not you want to settle for a lover who is dishonest to you, his live-in mate and most of all, untrue to himself. You must come to the conclusion as to whether or not you feel you deserve better.

While you are openly truthful about who you are, your bisexual lover is doing just the opposite. He is a coward hiding in his convenient "closet."

He has already threatened to "let you go." Don't wait for him to make that decision for you. Leave this confused cop, now!

All human beings deserve to be loved. You must find a mate who is well-grounded in his alternative lifestyle and can appreciate and love you for who you are.

FORGET THE QUICK-FIX FICTION LOVE

To make any relationship work, you must talk about your expectations first. You should marry your best friend. It's important to marry out of mutual support for each other's well-being. Many couples who have quickly fallen in love have just as rapidly fallen out of love. Love is not some ditch, pit, or bottomless well that you fall into. It takes mutual patience, trust, and compassion to make a compatible love relationship last.

PATIENCE IS A VIRTUE

Thirty-four-year-old Bonnie is a single mother of a four-year-old son. She was abandoned by the child's father during her second month of pregnancy; she had remained celibate since.

One day during a telephone conversation with her girlfriend, Andrea, who lives in Atlanta, Bonnie told Andrea that she had just about given up hope of ever meeting and marrying a decent black man. Andrea informed her that she knew a few eligible men in Atlanta. She told Bonnie about thirty-nine-year-old Ruben, who was her husband's cousin. She described him as being nice, single, successful, and sincere. At the close of their conversation, Andrea promised Bonnie she would give Ruben her number.

One week later, Bonnie received a call from Ruben. They connected with each other immediately. She told him she was studying to become a nurse. He said he was a managing director of an insurance company. They found out that they had a lot in common, and spoke to each other on a regular basis. They decided they were ideal for each other.

After four months of long-distance telephone courtship, Ruben flew up to Boston to spend Thanksgiving with Bonnie. They enjoyed each other's company. Bonnie spent Christmas with Ruben in Atlanta. On New Year's Day Ruben proposed to Bonnie. She accepted and started planning their wedding for the following July.

LOVE WITHOUT TRUST DON'T MEAN A THING, EVEN IF YOU'VE GOT THE RING

Bonnie was scheduled to complete her studies in December of the same year. Ruben suggested that they postpone the wedding until she finished her studies in Boston and was able to relocate to Atlanta. Then they would live together as husband and wife, instead of being married and living apart for the five months it would take her to complete her nursing program. She was very annoyed and disturbed about this. It caused constant arguments between them.

BONNIE: I don't want to wait. I've already started to plan the wedding. This is causing a major disagreement between us. All we do is argue about this all the time.

DR. CORNISH: This is not a good place to start from. If you are already in love with each other, what difference will a few more months make? It is more practical to extend your engagement and wait until you can relocate to get married.

BONNIE: But I don't want to wait any longer.

DR. CORNISH: Bonnie, are you afraid that he might change his mind?

BONNIE: Well, yes.

DR. CORNISH: If that's what you're worried about, then you really do need to wait and see if your relationship will pass the test of the extended engagement. Rushing in now will only give you a wedding; it will not guarantee a marriage. If you want to go the distance with your fiancé, I suggest you stop arguing about a wedding date and concentrate on building trust and respect together.

BONNIE: It's just not fair. Why should I have to wait?

DR. CORNISH: Bonnie, you're missing the point. You're the one who is not being fair. I understand your fear. You got a bad deal with your last relationship. You've been alone for a while, and now you've met someone whom you want to take care of you. And you're afraid that he might abandon you like your baby's father did. Bonnie, your fear is perfectly normal, but if this man loves you, he will stick around. But trying to force a premature wedding is not the way to go—believe me.

WIPE YOUR TEARS AND FACE YOUR TRUE FEARS

At the end of our conversation, Bonnie was still adamant about getting her fiancé to commit to the July wedding date. I hadn't heard from her for two months when she called to say she had gotten herself into a complicated predicament. Her baby's father, who had run out on her, had suddenly shown up from nowhere. This is the same man she'd been trying to track down for the past four years to get child support payments from, but she had been unable to get any help from him because the court could never find a permanent address for him. Now, after a long disappearing act, he had reappeared on the scene. He had asked for a second chance.

She said he had apologized for being "irresponsible and immature" in the past. But now he had gotten himself together, had a decent paying job, and wanted to start supporting his son. She said she had forgiven him and "spent time with him," and now she was "confused."

DR. CORNISH: What kind of time did you spend together—did you sleep with him?

BONNIE: *(Pause)* Well, yes.

DR. CORNISH: Are you still in love with him?

BONNIE: Yes, I am.

DR. CORNISH: What about your fiancé? Are you still in love with him, too?

BONNIE: I don't know. I don't think so . . . I'm not sure anymore.

DR. CORNISH: You've just answered the question right there. If you have to wonder if you are in love, then you're not in love. You said right away that you are still in love with your baby's father. So, he's the one you should be building a life with. If you don't really love your fiancé, the honest thing to do is to break the engagement.

BONNIE: I'm not sure if I want to do that. He can afford to provide a better life for me and my son. I have to . . .

You've Got to Face It, Before You Can Fix It

DR. CORNISH: Bonnie, what you're saying is that your heart is with your son's father, but you're using your fiancé because he has more money.

BONNIE: Not really.

DR. CORNISH: You have to be honest with yourself. If you're not being faithful to him now, why go through with the marriage? All the money in the world cannot buy you love. It's unfair for you to use this man like this. Why get hitched to one guy when you're in love with another? I think you know the right thing to do here. Don't you?

BONNIE: Yeah. Okay.

DR. CORNISH: Bonnie, marriage is a sacred bonding. Don't go into it if your heart isn't into it. It's a very important step. It doesn't make sense to do it with the wrong person and then end up resenting him, or visiting divorce court shortly after.

BONNIE: That's true . . . you're right.

LEARN TO COMMUNICATE BEFORE IT'S TOO LATE

It's truly surprising when couples won't take the time to talk with each other behind closed doors, but prefer to escape into the arms of someone else instead of working on what they already have with their spouses. One such case is that of twenty-eight-year-old LaToya, who appeared on an episode of *Ricki Lake* entitled "The Holidays Are Here, Ho! Ho! Ho! . . . But Sorry, Baby, You've Got to Go!"

The program was about people who wanted to break up with their spouses before Christmas. The holidays are usually when we celebrate family ties and give gifts. But the gift LaToya chose to give to her husband of four years, thirty-one-year-old David, was not what he expected:

HE BLAMES/SHE BLAMES

LaToya told David that when they first got married things had been "smooth sailing." She said that he used to be passionate, caring, and loving, but that as time had passed, he had become less romantic and less interested in her. She felt lonely and frustrated because he was never at home. And now she had found someone, a "special friend," who was compassionate and spent time with her.

She blames: "You don't spend time with me, and I just want to go my way, and I want you to go yours before Christmas."

David was surprised and hurt by LaToya's revelation. He told her that he was never at home because he spent all his time working overtime to take care of her and their three-year-old daughter. He said he was trying to earn enough money to buy them a new home and to pay the high credit-card bills for her excessive shopping. He felt stressed-out and frustrated because he was always at work. He said he couldn't believe she was busy cheating on him while he was busy working to build a better life for them.

He blames: "You're complaining about love and affection? I'm working two jobs to support your shopaholic habit. You can go your own way."

As the show progressed, I helped the couple to stop blaming each other and to speak openly with each other. They both realized that they weren't paying attention to each other's feelings at home. As the dialogue continued, LaToya realized she had made a mistake by turning to another man for comfort, and she wanted a second chance. Unfortunately, David said that because of LaToya's infidelity he wouldn't be able to trust her again, and that the marriage was over.

Had the couple communicated openly with each other and tried to see each other's viewpoint before the infidelity, this marriage could have been saved.

IF YOU WANT A GOOD RELATIONSHIP, YOU'VE GOT TO WORK ON IT

All relationships take patience and communication. The very same communication you shared in the beginning is what will make your marriage last. Frequently, sisters pull the "quick change" act as soon as they cross the threshold. The problem is we expect a quick fix. We want relationships to come ready-made. They don't. Relationships take work. Statistics reveal that seven out of every ten black marriages quickly end in divorce. This is very frightening.

A common mistake many black couples make is that we expect to have a perfect relationship just because we happen to share the same ethnic background. This is one of the biggest misconceptions we harbor. Having similar ethnicity is a good foundation. But, *compatible love* has to be built upon this foundation to make the relationship last.

The essence of compatible love is explained in depth in my previous book *Radiant Women of Color:* "Compatible love does not come overnight. It has to be built. It involves consideration for each other's feelings. Compatibility entails passing love's difficult tests—overcoming selfishness, false pride, and unforgiv-ingness. It is not always easy, but should always be kind—not always exciting, but should always be warm. Sometimes it requires putting aside your own desires to accommodate your companion's. It is a trade-off, a compromise. There must be a healthy balance between the minds, bodies, and spirits of both people involved."

I surveyed two hundred brothers and asked them to candidly share some of the things that have broken up their relationships. I asked them to be realistic and honest, and not to view this as a sister-bashing arena, but as a thought-provoking forum to help us develop better communication with each other. Here is what they shared:

THE TEN TABOOS THAT TEAR RELATIONSHIPS APART

1. Bombarding — Not giving him enough space.
2. Masquerading — Acting innocent and sweet in the beginning, then suddenly changing.
3. Parading — Showing off and competing with him to prove how tough, independent, and smart you are.
4. Withholding — Refusing to have sex with him; using it as a means to spite him.
5. Cheating — Having affairs behind his back.
6. Fronting — Not saying exactly what you mean; poor communication.
7. Hoarding — Wanting him to buy you too many things.
8. Referencing — Always talking about other men or old boyfriends.
9. Freezing — Being cold and harsh toward him.
10. Nagging — Constantly complaining about everything, even insignificant things.

MARRY A FRIEND, NOT A FANTASY

Sis, relationships are too important to be taken for granted. Let's break the illusion of the soap-opera version, and go for the compatible real-life version.

The key to long-lasting love relationships is: Marry your best friend, communicate honestly, respect your mate, and above all, be kind to yourself.

epilogue

I recently gave a seminar and discussion called "Black Male/Female Relationships: How to Have a Successful Love Life!" The turnout was amazing. It was a sold-out, standing-room-only event. But what I found most fascinating was the ratio of men to women who attended.

There was actually an equal balance of black men and black women who came to this seminar. This is a good sign. There was a time when you could not catch a man in public talking about his feelings. I'm happy to report that these brothers who attended came seeking answers and opened themselves to dialogue with the sisters who were present.

However, there was one egocentric fellow who was only too proud to volunteer his "homemade expertise" when a sister asked, "Why do men cheat?"

"I have the answer to that one," he boasted. "You see, when we [men] first get together with you [women], it's challenging. So we make sure we do everything to get you hooked and keep you happy. We do all the right moves [sexually], and when we know we satisfy you, and you can't let go, we get tired and want a new challenge."

"But what does it take for a man to be satisfied with one woman?" the sister asked.

At this point, cheered on by one of his sidekicks, he bragged, "It's hard for any one woman to satisfy a man. It's our nature to go hunting for new adventure, just like in the caveman days. You have to allow us to be who we are. After a while we get bored when you can't keep up. We go looking for new excitement. It's not cheating, it's just a man's thing—"

"That's nonsense!" I interrupted. "This is not about the caveman era. The rest of us are here in civilized time, and that's what this seminar is about. Since you brought up sex, let's talk about it. You claim men cheat because women can't keep up with them in bed. That's ridiculous, because if the truth be told here, no man can out-sex a woman if she puts her mind to it. Women's bodies are designed by nature for prolonged performance, while men have to stop and refuel." The sisters in the room applauded this response. "As a matter of fact," I continued, "a lot of women fake orgasms because they don't want to hurt the man's feelings. So stop using sex as an excuse, because most of the time, it is the woman who is not satisfied by the man's performance."

"No way," he said.

"It's true. I faked it once," said one sister.

"Me too," added another. This began a chain reaction of "me too" confessions throughout the room.

The tables were now turned. The men wanted to know why women "faked." This brought forth a healthy interchange of dialogue between the brothers and sisters. They spoke openly and honestly in a safe and nurturing environment. The men and women realized they had a lot of similar experiences and fears.

To sum it up, they found out that they were looking for the same thing: All were just trying to make it in life—striving to be fulfilled in friendships and relationships and to earn enough money to live without worry.

Sis, I'll leave you with this: All of us have made some bad choices in the past. There's nothing wrong with making a mistake. What's detrimental is if you ignore or refuse to correct the bad choices. Deal with your situation right where you are today. Admonish yourself, "I'm getting out of this frame because I don't like the picture." You are not a victim—you have a choice. Therefore, you are empowered.

Black men are not your enemy. You may have chosen a few

bad apples, but they don't spoil the whole bunch. You are not to be blamed for someone else's shortcomings, but you must take full responsibility for your own actions.

Make it your responsibility to yourself to truly *like* the individual who you are. Choose wisely—invest in you, and you will overcome any problems in life. Make the commitment to *become the best you that you can be,* and you will truly be blessed.

You deserve happiness, sis. Don't deprive yourself. I'm in your corner.

Go for it!

referrals

Here's a listing of twenty-one toll-free numbers that you may find helpful:

1. Women for Sobriety   (800)333-1606
2. Center for Substance Abuse Prevention   (800)729-6686
3. National Council on Alcohol and Drug
   Dependence   (800)475-HOPE
4. American Cancer Society   (800)ACS-2345
5. American Heart Association   (800)242-8721
6. American Diabetes Association   (800)ADA-DISC
7. Domestic Violence Hotline   (800)942-6906
8. End Abuse Helpline   (800)END-ABUS
9. National Domestic Abuse Helpline   (800)799-7233
10. Planned Parenthood Federation
    of America   (800)829-7732
11. Planned Parenthood Family   (800)230-PLAN
12. Pregnancy Helpline   (800)238-4269
13. National Sexually Transmitted
    Disease Hotline   (800)227-8922
14. Depression Awareness, Recognition
    and Treatment   (800)421-4211
15. National Family & Children Mental
    Health Support   (800)628-1696
16. The Center for Disease Control (CDC)
    National AIDS Hotline   (800)342-AIDS
17. National Organization for Victim
    Assistance   (800)TRY-NOVA

18. National Child Abuse Hotline   (800)422-4453
19. National Council on Family Violence   (800)223-6004
20. Pre-paid Legal Services®   (800)645-7757
21. Consumer Credit Repair Services   (800)284-1723

For information about Dr. Cornish's *SISTERS ON THE MOVE®* seminar series, speaking engagements, workshops, training programs, audiotapes, or to schedule her for a presentation, contact:

Dr. Grace Cornish
Cornish Worldwide Productions
610 Fifth Ave — P.O. Box 4739
New York, NY 10185-0040
(212)576-8811; FAX (212)489-6399

You can also learn more about Dr. Cornish's work and/or order her other books and tapes from her World Wide Web Site at:

http://www.drgcornish@aol.com